SOMETHING TO Think ABOUT

Making Sense of Faith,
Prayer, Creation and a
Whole Lot More

R.M. DE GARIS

SOMETHING TO THINK ABOUT
Copyright © 2015 by R.M. De Garis

All dictionary definitions taken from the New Lexicon Webster's Dictionary of the English Language, Encyclopedic Edition (New York, NY: Lexicon Publications, 1988), edited by Bernard S. Cayne.

ISBN: 978-1-4866-0742-6   Printed in Canada

Word Alive Press
131 Cordite Road, Winnipeg, MB R3W 1S1
www.wordalivepress.ca

MIX
Paper from responsible sources
FSC® C016245

Library and Archives Canada Cataloguing in Publication

De Garis, R. M., 1950-, author
  Something to think about / R.M. De Garis.

Issued in print and electronic formats.
ISBN 978-1-4866-0742-6 (pbk.).--ISBN 978-1-4866-0743-3 (pdf).--
ISBN 978-1-4866-0744-0 (html).--ISBN 978-1-4866-0745-7 (epub)

1. Kingdom of God--Prayers and devotions. 2. Christian life--Meditations. I. Title.

BS680.K52D4 2015   236   C2015-903124-9
                                         C2015-903125-7

Dedicated to the Etterbeek, Brussels home group.
Their questions were the inspiration for *Something to Think About!*

In memory of Maureen Barnett,
who opened her heart and her home to the group.

Contents

Foreword

I am very pleased that this small volume has found its way into your home, and I pray that it may in some small way assist you in learning to be a citizen of the Kingdom of Heaven.

A few years back, my wife Sandy and I hosted a weekly Bible study in our home. *Something to Think About* originated as an addendum to the notice regarding the weekly agenda I sent out. After a few months, the repetitive writing of time, topic, and special activities became tedious. It seemed logical, since I was writing anyway, to add a short dialogue on any thought that caught my mind at the time. The intent was then, and is now, to help ordinary folks like you and I grow by encouraging them to think through the various components of their faith.

I am not a theologian. I never graduated from Bible College, a Christian university, or any university at all for that matter. My knowledge of the Bible has been learnt through sixty-odd years of sermons from a dozen or more dedicated ministers of the gospel, and through my own reading of the Scriptures. I should also give credit to Christian Service Brigade. I have heard the scriptural and doctrinal portion of their achievement programme compared to a year's Bible college training; having completed said programme, I can testify to its thoroughness. By the time I completed the doctrinal and scripture requirements, there were very few books in the Bible I had not read, analysed, and written about.

My chosen occupation is—or I should say, was—air traffic control. I served for over thirty years in an operational capacity before hanging up my headset. I spent the next ten years working in advanced planning before finally retiring four years ago. Now I drive a truck, which has given me a lot of time to think. What has all this to do with this book? Plenty, actually!

Air traffic controllers are free thinkers by nature. We have to be able to identify a problem, evaluate possible solutions, and come up with the right answer—all within a few seconds. We have to do all this while communicating instructions to other aircraft, planning the sequence and content of the next several transmissions, and listening to adjacent sector controllers hand over incoming or accept outgoing flights we have previously placed in the hand-off mode. There is no room for error. The end result: controllers seldom take anything for granted but continually question until they are certain they have the correct solution.

Each topic presented herein is a result of a question. Sometimes the questions originated from one of our home group members. Sometimes the questions originated in my own mind, but always the solutions are found in Scripture.

Although the thoughts expressed in *Something to think about!* are Biblically sound, they may not necessarily represent the popular interpretation—and that is more than okay. Whilst I didn't set out to write a contrary opinion to every paragraph in my favourite commentaries, this occurred frequently enough that I was forced to evaluate every area of faith, resulting in a stronger and more firmly seated foundation. Paul's comment regarding the Berean Christians is as valid today as it was two thousand years ago: he commended them for questioning all teaching and for persistently examining Scripture to ensure that the teaching they were receiving was Biblically sound. For myself, I have learnt that if I read without questioning, I seldom discover new ideas.

Two Additional Items

There are several chapters that deal with evolutionary issues. Just as I have no formal training in apologetics, so too my training has not included any of the sciences. The scientific information contained within these chapters is basic: it is not rocket science and does not require a doctorate to understand.

Several chapters will introduce the reader to a member of the congregation named Third Pew. Both he and the pastor to whom he writes are fictitious. This technique was chosen as a means to introduce specific theological or church-related topics in a manner that adds variety. Hopefully you will find these folks to be informative. Enjoy.

I pray that each page you turn will, as the title says, give you *something to think about!*

Chapter 1

A Cup of Coffee

AFTER YOUR SALVATION, WHAT WOULD YOU CONSIDER TO BE THE MOST valuable gift God has given you? While you ponder that one, continue reading.

Whenever a group of professionals gets together in a break room for coffee, it won't be long before they start telling stories—some true, some they wish were true, and some that are legend within the profession. Then it's only a matter of time before the talk turns to problems at work, problems with management, and problems at home as a result of work. Traffic, commuting problems, cost of parking—all seem to contribute to the general discontent. I suspect that each of us has participated in such a discussion.

Most kitchens contain about eight matching cups and saucers. After that, there are a few chipped china mugs, some odd cups from Aunt Martha, and a couple of twenty-five-cent spares from the dollar store. When folks come over for coffee and the dishes are put out on the table, the matching ones are taken first, whilst those old chipped and battered mugs are inevitably everybody's last choice. Those who reluctantly accept those mugs look rather enviously upon those who, arriving first, have grabbed the best dishes.

Now, what does the second paragraph have to do with the first? The second will hopefully provide the key to reducing or even eliminating the stress created by those problems mentioned in the first paragraph.

The purpose of the professional's gathering is to relax and enjoy a cup of coffee. Take it from one who enjoys his coffee: the quality of the container has no bearing whatsoever on the quality of the coffee. Yet some of those with less expensive cups may frown as they consider their utilitarian containers and contrast them with the more ornate vessels being held by their compatriots, who obtained them simply because they arrived first. The late arrivals may behave as though they have somehow been given an inferior product, robbing them of the full joy of the moment.

By now I'm certain you're wondering what on earth I'm talking about, but please keep reading. It will all become clear.

Life is the coffee, and the jobs, houses, cars, possessions, money, and position in society are the cups. They are just tools to hold and contain life, and the type of cup we have doesn't define or change the quality of life we live. Sometimes, by concentrating only on the cup, we fail to enjoy the coffee God has provided us. God brews the coffee, not the cups.

Do the math! There are 8,760 hours in a year (twenty-four hours multiplied by 365 day). Given four weeks of vacation time per year, plus two additional weeks for government approved holidays (ten days), and taking into account two hours for commuting per day, you spend 2,300 hours working every year (fifty hours multiplied by forty-six weeks). That leaves 6,460 hours for family, friends, and hobbies—and eating and sleeping, of course. Yet which part of your life (work or home) occupies the greatest amount of your planning and is considered the most valuable?

I would be willing to bet that your fondest memory of childhood revolves around family or friendship, not the size of your parents' paycheques or the status of their places of employment.

In Genesis, we read that we were placed upon the earth with a role to subjugate it, not to be dominated by it. This includes time. So take a moment today to talk to friends, play with the kids, enjoy the flowers, and taste the coffee.

Something to think about!

Chapter 2

You Are Welcome

Dear Third Pew,

Isn't it amazing how hard we struggle to convert a simple, joyful plan for living into drudgery? Both the New and Old Testaments echo with words like joy, peace, longevity (read the Psalms), prosperity, and happiness, yet we Christians delight in selecting passages that appear to focus on work or suffering and pain and say that these are the characteristics of those who will be part of the Kingdom of Heaven. Since the Sermon on the Mount is the longest direct quotation of Jesus' teaching, and since the Beatitudes are the introductory statements to this sermon, your observation would be cause to question what the rest of Scripture says is a good life. That is, if what you wrote was correct. I can assure you it isn't.

Jesus' second most important role whilst on earth, after providing our means of rejoining His Father's Kingdom as fully redeemed citizens, was that of being a teacher. To a teacher, the primary indicator of a successful lesson is when a behavioural change is witnessed in the class. Jesus was a superb teacher who used common issues of the day and statements made by His audience as starting points for the change He wished to see. The Sermon on the Mount was delivered to bring hope and joy to a group of poverty-stricken peasants who were taxed to death by the Romans and sneered at by their own rulers and scholars—the scribes, Pharisees, and church leaders. His primary purpose in teaching was to convey the message that the Kingdom was here and now (Matthew 4:17).

In order to do that. He had to first convince His audience that what He was about to say was relevant to them. He was successful, too. Here's what the people said at the conclusion of the sermon: *"He taught them as one having authority, and not as the scribes"* (Matthew 7:29).

Since His lesson was geared to the students present at the time, before we look at the lesson itself we have to look at the makeup of the group. From Matthew 4:24, we find that they *"brought to Him all sick people who were afflicted with various diseases and torments, and those who were demon-possessed, epileptics, and paralytics; and He healed them."* Our audience is composed of sick people and their relatives. Others in the crowd would have been the unemployed, street people, curiosity seekers attracted by the noise, and a few representatives of the local synagogue. A few middle-class folks would have wondered what all the noise was about as well. Most of these folks were probably poor, since sick people can't work. There was no social security, and their relatives had to support them.

In the Palestine of the first century, church folks were the rich and educated class. Being rich was equated with being holy, since God had obviously blessed you. Disease was an indicator that sin was buried somewhere in your life. John 9 tells of a man born blind, about whom the disciples asked Jesus, *"Rabbi, who sinned, this man or his parents, that he was born blind?"* (John 9:2)

There was an entire sub-culture of ritualistic cleanliness that had to be followed to worship in the temple. Otherwise you were limited to one of the outer courtyards. Remember the man who was robbed in the parable of the Good Samaritan? One reason the church leaders had for walking clear of him was to avoid coming into contact with uncleanness (blood and open sores) that would prevent them from participating in worship. How often do you think a working man from the fields or factories would be free of open cuts, bruises, and be able to take the time to cleanse himself as the law required so that he could be a part of temple worship?

So, keeping in mind the audience and the culture, and remembering that the primary goal of the lesson was to present the Kingdom to the group present, I'll paraphrase the lesson: "God's Kingdom is here and now, and because of Me you can have access to it. It doesn't matter to Me whether you are miserable, poor, beat-up, spiritually down, hungry, or abused. You are all welcome in God's Kingdom, *regardless of your personal situation.* For those who think that money, influence, social standing, or church affiliation will get you in, forget it. I am the way, the truth, and the life and no one can approach the Father except through Me."

You see, the Sermon on the Mount is all about citizenship in the Kingdom. It's all about Jesus. There is nothing spiritually uplifting about being hungry, poor, or abused. Being poor and miserable isn't a passport to Heaven. Jesus isn't saying that wealth and happiness bring condemnation. There is nothing wrong with being rich, happy, or healthy, provided these don't prevent you from meeting God. What He's saying is: "Do not worry about your life, what you will eat or drink, but seek first the Kingdom of God and you will find it." And there are no exclusions.

In summary, status won't buy admittance and the lack of something to wear to church won't keep you out. Heaven's gates will open to all who look for them. The Beatitudes are not a list of qualifications for Heaven. You could write your own list if you wanted to. How about these: "Blessed is the drunkard, for he shall become intoxicated with joy"? Or maybe "Blessed is the lonely soul who hides in his room, for he shall stand in the Heavenly choir"? Or finally, "Blessed are the parents who watch with pride as their children grow in their knowledge of the Lord, for they shall spend eternity remembering that joy"?

Remember what the writer said about Abraham: that the people would call him blessed. He certainly didn't fit into any of the Beatitude categories. The Bible says, *"For everyone who asks receives, and he who seeks finds, and to him who knocks it will be opened"* (Matthew 7:8). We are all blessed!

Something to think about!

Chapter 3

The Living Book

IN 1971, AN ILLINOIS BUSINESSMAN BY THE NAME OF KENNETH TAYLOR published a modern English paraphrase of the Bible that he entitled *The Living Bible*. Even though I've had a copy sitting on my bookshelf ever since, I have never given the title much thought. It was just another version to go with my NASB, my NIV, and my NKJV. I find that it's useful as a reference tool even though it isn't a properly accredited translation. I suspect that there are a large number of forty-somethings out there who, if they search their closets and attics, will rediscover their own copy; it was a favourite handout for evangelical young people's groups and teen Sunday school classes in the late 60s (for the New Testament) and the early 70s.

But this isn't about the Bible itself. It's the title I got to thinking about.

> *For the* word *of God is living and powerful, and sharper than any two-edged sword, piercing even to the division of soul and spirit, and of joints and marrow, and is a discerner of the thoughts and intents of the heart. And there is no creature hidden from His sight, but all things are naked and open to the eyes of Him to whom we must give account.*
>
> —Hebrews 4:12–13 (emphasis added)

> *In the beginning was the* Word, *and the* Word *was with God, and the* Word *was God; this one was in the beginning with God; all things through him did happen, and without him happened not even*

one thing that hath happened. In him was life, and the life was the light of men...

—John 1:1–4, YLT (emphasis added)

I wondered, how can a book be considered alive? So out came Webster. I'm going to walk you through the definitions I went through without comment—at least not until the end. First off, of course, we start with the word "living."

> **Living: the condition of having life.**
>
> **Life: the state of an organism characterized by certain processes or abilities...**
>
> **Organism: Any living being or its material structure... Any complete whole, which by the integration, interaction and mutual dependence of its parts is comparable to a living being.**

Think about any living entity you may be familiar with and see how the definitions listed above are fulfilled. It doesn't matter whether it's a plant, baboon, human, or crow.

Now take that living entity and remove a piece. The organism is impaired and unable to function properly. Birds require two wings to fly. Two eyes help prevent us from being blindsided while driving. Without petals, flowers cannot attract the insects required for pollination. Each part depends upon the others for survival, for replication, or for aesthetics. Each part also has a specific position within the organism and interacts with the other parts in a specific manner. Most organisms can survive the loss of a few bits and pieces and continue to function, albeit somewhat impaired in movement or appearance, but take enough bits away and it will no longer function as intended. Remove a few more bits and the organism will die.

Now think about your Bible and apply the same rationale as you did with the examples above. The Bible is no different—with one exception, which we will get to in a moment. It's a complete whole, from

Genesis to Revelation. Each chapter reinforces the message being conveyed by the complete Word. The Gospels interact with the prophets, with the life of Christ providing the fulfillment to many of them. Paul's letters draw upon the books of the law and the prophets to complete their logical arguments for the reality of our salvation and heavenly citizenship. Genesis provides the beginnings whilst the prophecies in Revelation bring this earth to its ending and new beginning.

If you take away certain parts, the story becomes incomplete. Think what the effect would be if John 20 were removed! How about Matthew 1? Surely it would be possible to eliminate all those begats. Removing Revelation would eliminate many of the objections people have concerning Scripture. Controversial areas like Genesis 1 or Job 40 could be left out of the new publication, thus assuring acceptance by all critics.

In fact, the politically correct version of the NIV hit the newsstands in 2006. The new version of the Sacred Scriptures was presented at a book fair in Frankfurt. Subtitled *The Bible in a More Just Language,* the so-called translation has Jesus no longer referring to God as "Father," but as "our Mother and Father who are in heaven." Likewise, Jesus is no longer referred to as the "Son" but rather as the "child" of God. The title "Lord" is replaced with "God" or "the Eternal One." The devil, however, is still referred to with masculine pronouns.

In December 2005, Matin Dreyer, pastor and founder of the sect "Jesus Freaks," published the "Volksbibel" (The People's Bible) in a supposed attempt to make the message of Christianity more accessible. Jesus "returns" instead of resurrects, and it multiplies "hamburgers" instead of fishes and loaves. In the parable of the prodigal son, the younger son squanders his inheritance at dance clubs and ends up cleaning bathrooms at McDonald's.

Before we leave this portion of the argument, the difference between the Word and all other organisms is that the Word is eternal. You can burn it, ban it, bury it, deface it, or ridicule it, but you cannot stop its message from being broadcast throughout the world. It *cannot* be slain.

Oftentimes we consider the Word as being the story of God's interaction with man, and I would certainly not attempt to argue against this definition, but to my mind it seems a bit incomplete. The Word is ever so much more than a simple biography. No biography serves any purpose other than to acquaint the reader with the subject of the biography. It's true that we may learn some significant lessons from reading specific biographies, but those lessons are secondary to the main purpose of the biography.

The Word has a number of very specific functions in addition to relaying the story of God and man. Several are identified in the Hebrews 4 reference quoted at the start of this chapter. The sword image here is not the two-handed broadsword of King Arthur fame, nor is it the curved scimitar as used by Aladdin; rather, it's the short fighting sword used by the Greeks in close combat. It would be approximately the size of a dagger. From days long past when I worked in a butcher's shop, I can assure you that cutting through a joint to separate the limb from the torso requires an extremely sharp and flexible blade. It also requires a great deal of skill to penetrate the joint and separate the ball and socket so that the two parts are divided cleanly. Joints are hard to divide. A cleaver or axe won't cut through cleanly. Only an expertly wielded blade can do it.

The purpose of this precision cutting is to expose man's inner heart. This is done not to encourage ridicule or promote pain, but to reveal to us those things that must be excised if growth and spiritual good health is to prevail. The Word exposes our hearts, and then, if we acknowledge its findings, it enables us to claim God's promises. These are the two edges!

Do you wonder about the difference between the soul and the spirit? The spirit is the intelligent (or immaterial) part of man. The soul is the eternal. So the Word distinguishes between the stuff that's nice to know and useful to correct to get along in this world and the things we need to fix in light of eternity.

We don't need to worry about defeating the opposition, because the Word is all-powerful. Besides, waging war is not our job. Jesus said, *"All power is given unto me in heaven and in earth"* (Matthew 28:18, KJV).

Speaking of power, that's another function of the Living Word. Because the Word is alive, it's able to respond on its own and in the most appropriate manner. Our task is simply to call upon the Word for

assistance and then believe that the promised help will be f
ing. That's what Jesus did. Recall if you would the account t
temptation. In response to each attack, Jesus drew upon the written
Word and let that Word stand as his only response.

As to the means by which the Word provides assistance, Ephesians 6 provides the details. The shield is a defensive bulwark. Using it
effectively simply requires the defender to position the shield between
his body and the enemy and hold it steady. No skills required. The
sword is the means for striking back.

The early church, in the third century, attributed the writing of
Hebrews to Paul, although scholars today aren't so sure. Whoever the
author is, his selection of words was very specific. We all know that
Paul was a Pharisee before he became a believer. One of the less en-
dearing traits of the Pharisees was their tendency to become bogged
down in very specific arguments. They were schooled in the art of
debating and creating airtight legal arguments. Engaging in philosophical arguments on issues such as how many angels can dance on
the head of a pin, identifying the length of a Sabbath day walk, or determining the means by which a man could shirk his responsibility to
care for his aged parents taught them to carefully select the most appropriate words. The verb used by the author of Hebrews to describe
the work of the Word is most specific. It is the Word that *pierces* and
discerns, not any outside force wielding it.

I have one last thought. We believe in the Trinity: God in three
persons. Hebrews states that the Word is alive. John 1 takes this life
one step further and states that the Word is not only alive, but that it is
God. Jesus is that Word and He declared that He had been granted all
power, and furthermore He would make sure He was with us.

Feeling tempted? Feeling a little down this morning? All you
have to do is call upon the Word, and then have faith and believe that
God Himself can do the job of defending you.

Now, *that's* something to think about!

Chapter 4

Why Not the Church?

Dear Pastor,

My wife and I spent last Sunday visiting with my brother-in-law, and so we went to their service on Sunday. I was impressed. They have two morning services now, one at 9:30 and the other at 11:00 just to accommodate all the folks that are attending. Just about everyone who's gone missing from our services here was there, and the same goes for a number of folks from the Baptist and the Presbyterian congregations.

Me and the wife got to wondering on the way home why that should be. I mean, our music is just as good as theirs, and you're certainly as good a talker as their man, so why should all the folks have migrated over there? Why is their church growing in such great numbers whilst ours just goes up by ones and twos? Do we need to add a gym or get a music director or what? Whatever it is, just let me know and I'll get the board working on it first thing the next meeting.

Sincerely yours,

Third Pew Back, Left-Hand Side

Dear Third Pew,

I'm more than a little disappointed in your question today, but since you are offering to help, maybe you should provide a bit of encouragement to the younger members to come out on Wednesday nights. Apart from that, I can't think of anything that we need to do differently.

So why am I disappointed? There are a couple of verses you should consider:

> *So continuing daily with one accord in the temple, and breaking bread from house to house, they ate their food with gladness and simplicity of heart, praising God and having favor with all the people. And the Lord added to the church daily those who were being saved.*
>
> —Acts 2:46–47

> *Then the word of God spread, and the number of the disciples multiplied greatly in Jerusalem, and a great many of the priests were obedient to the faith.*
>
> —Acts 6:7

According to Scripture, Christ's church doesn't grow by having the Smiths move from the Baptist to the Anglican building. That isn't growth, that's just a rearrangement of chairs. When folks change churches whilst remaining in the same town, it is generally because:

- the church they're attending has changed its focus and they just can't agree with the new direction.
- they've had an argument with one or more of the dominant cliques within the church.
- they feel that they're in need of programmes that aren't being offered at their previous church.
- they're afraid of making a commitment, and changing venues enables them to avoid getting involved.

Although a pastor is always glad to welcome new folks into the family, he does so with the awareness that these folks are hurting in some way. He's not welcoming a newly created saint but rather battered believers who definitely are in need of prayer, probably require comforting, and possibly need counselling.

Consider the quoted verses! When we see unsaved friends and neighbours kneel in confession that Jesus Christ is Lord, we're witnessing scriptural church growth. When we witness our fellow believers queuing up for a seat for a scheduled evening of prayer and Bible study, we're witnessing scriptural church growth. When we see people healed and prayers being answered, we're witnessing scriptural church growth.

Unfortunately, very few churches are growing. The figure is a dismal one percent for growth in evangelical churches in North America. Sadly, that means most churches that do grow are growing because of believer migration. So if one church is growing, it means another is declining, and that isn't what God intended at all.

The church has lost its influence. Nobody pays attention to it anymore. The legislation of governments past sustained or built upon the church's moral code, even though its authors might not have believed in God. Schools taught Christian ethics and behaviour. Not anymore!

In a desperate bid to attract "sinners," churches have developed programmes for youth, hired music directors, installed elaborate sound systems, and instead of sermons now offer homilies complete with coffee and donuts. Church statements-of-belief have been carefully edited to avoid offending. Churches are no longer churches but corporations, in this manner avoiding litigation should something said or done within its walls cause offence. But instead of attracting outsiders, all they have succeeded in doing is raiding the pews of the denomination down the street.

Take a look at 1 Peter 2:7–8:

Unto you therefore which believe he is precious: but unto them which be disobedient, the stone which the builders disallowed, the same is made the head of the corner, and a stone of stumbling, and a rock of offence, even to them which stumble at the word, being disobedient... (KJV)

If Christ himself is an offence to those who don't believe, the church (His creation) shouldn't be trying to change this image. In fact, I believe that our placating manner is one reason why we are failing to attract sinners. All our adaptation and modernization appears to be repelling them—and when you think about it, it makes sense.

Blessed are you when they revile and persecute you, and say all kinds of evil against you falsely for My sake. Rejoice and be exceedingly glad, for great is your reward in heaven, for so they persecuted the prophets who were before you. You are the salt of the earth; but if the salt loses its flavor, how shall it be seasoned? It is then good for nothing but to be thrown out and trampled underfoot by men. You are the light of the world. A city that is set on a hill cannot be hidden.

—Matthew 5:11-14

We should be making the people around us jealous. We should walk with a bounce in our step and a smile on our faces. We should be driving people nuts with our outlook on life. It is this confident dependence upon God that causes people to want to tear us down. They want it, they know it's missing in their lives, and they're just plain jealous of us because we have what they need. Even whilst they're trying to negate our testimony, they are unfortunately aware that their own lives are brighter and more enjoyable because of us.

That is the salt and light that we add to this world. It isn't our youth programmes or our music or our scintillating sermons that attract sinners to our churches. It isn't our friendly dispositions or fresh donuts either. Municipal governments run better youth programmes, my favourite radio station has better music, and if I want someone to preach at me I can always talk to my mother (just kidding, honest). For social activities, my country club serves better coffee and the conversation there can often be quite stimulating. But none of these other venues can offer prayer or solutions for the heartaches I feel.

My dear Third Pew, re-read Acts 2. When was the last time you felt that you just couldn't wait to have dinner with the Smiths or Widow Jones, or to join Brother Iris on a Saturday afternoon for prayer, instead of going to the ballgame? Churches grow when the people eagerly gather together to pray and fellowship. Growing churches are marked by answered prayer and the evidence of the Holy Spirit at work (in other words, miracles) on a level that borders on routine. Growing churches expect growth. Churches grow because the individuals within them are alive and show it.

I thank you, however, for raising the question. If the subject of growth is causing you concern, I'm certain that it's bothering others as well. I will certainly address it. God bless you and we will see you Sunday in the third pew back, left-hand side.

Something to think about!

Chapter 5

Symptoms of a Growing Church

THERE IS ONE THING A GOOD SERMON OR LESSON SHOULD ALWAYS DO: LEAVE the listener with the desire to learn more. By that definition, the preceding Dear Pastor letter received a passing grade, as it stimulated the following questions:

1. It's all very well and good to talk about a growing church, but how do we actually apply the fertilizer to start the process?
2. How do we get the church back to basics?
3. Indeed, what are the biblical identification marks of a growing church?
4. What are these basics?

It's so easy to ask these questions, but coming up with answers is another story. Whatever the end result, let's take a look at these questions—one at a time.

Getting the Church Back to Basics

And through the hands of the apostles many signs and wonders were done among the people. And they were all with one accord in Solomon's Porch. Yet none of the rest dared join them, but the people esteemed them highly. And believers were increasingly added to the Lord, multitudes of both men and women...

—Acts 5:12–14

The average Christian's normal approach to problems is to first attempt to resolve it on their own, only calling out to Christ when things are so hopelessly confused that they can see no way out of it. It seems to me that we do the same thing as a collective body of believers when it comes to church. In our prayer lives, we tend to provide God with the end result we have decided is appropriate and then ask Him to endorse it and make it happen.

The church recognizes that it has a problem. It even identifies the problem correctly. As the question posed in the last chapter implies, the church admits that it needs to get back to basics, that the message of the church has strayed from the gospel. In response, the minister or board will organize revival meetings to follow directly after a special week of prayer. They will bring in guest speakers and special music. People will walk the aisle and get saved, but at the end of it all there will be little change.

Whilst the new names added to God's Book of Life may seem to make the whole exercise worthwhile, wouldn't it be wonderful if the same effort also produced a fire in the hearts of each believer in attendance? That's what happened in the early church and during the so-called Welsh revivals and at numerous other times during the church's history. Yet for some reason we have to re-learn the same lesson over and over: by ourselves we can do nothing. Every revival has been the result of prayer, not of planning.

Throughout the summers of 2011 and 2012, the news was full of stories regarding the Occupy Wall Street movement and its franchise protests in New York, in Venezuela, in Egypt... and for that matter in practically every major city one can name. Indeed, it is likely that one occurred in a city near you. I know there was one in Toronto. If you had asked most of the individuals why they were protesting and what they were seeking to accomplish, they probably would not be able to give you a coherent answer. But they were united in the idea that they had to be there.

Strangely enough, that's what God wants you to do in the church: be there, I mean. Follow me through the chain of events in Acts.

These all continued with one accord in prayer and supplication, with the women and Mary the mother of Jesus, and with His brothers.

—Acts 1:14

Notice that the disciples are all together, meeting in prayer and pleading. There's no indication of the focus of their prayer, but I think we can make a good guess. These are people who took lessons in prayer from Jesus Himself, so I suspect the themes outlined in the Disciple's Prayer (Lord's Prayer) would have been their focal point. Jesus spent three years teaching them about the Kingdom of Heaven. He taught about citizenship and the Kingdom lifestyle. Is it too much of a reach to propose that the disciples were focussed on the words from the Lord's Prayer? *"Thy Kingdom come. Thy will be done..."* (Luke 11:2, KJV) After all, Jesus had just left them with the command to go out and teach the lessons that He had taught.

The disciples set about replacing Judas in order to fulfill Scripture following the first session of prayer, and I suspect as a direct result of their conversations with God.

For it is written in the book of Psalms: "Let his dwelling place be desolate, and let no one live in it"; and, "Let another take his office."

—Acts 1:20 (emphasis added)

Then came Pentecost! The day started off with all the disciples (the previous chapter indicates that there were about 120) meeting together and in total agreement. But there's no indication that they had the day planned. Instead they were waiting and probably praying together. It's possible that they were in one of the temple courtyards since 120 people would require a fair amount of space, but we don't know that for sure.

Following the coming of the Holy Spirit, it would seem that each person started talking to people around him/her in that person's own language, so it seems likely that they were in the temple. Their conversation was entirely focused upon the wonderful works of God (Acts 2:11). When this witness had gone on for a while, Peter attracted the attention of all those around him and started to speak. His words centred entirely upon the executed and resurrected Jesus Christ.

Following Pentecost, the church continued to grow in leaps and bounds, and each growth spurt is described in the same manner—Bible study and fellowship, prayer, and unity of purpose and possessions. And what lessons were the apostles and disciples teaching? The same lessons that Jesus Himself, supported by Old Testament Scripture, had taught them would have been central to all apostolic teaching. The letters by James, Peter, and John would have been quite typical: all backed up by Old Testament quotes and all describing different facets of living in the Kingdom.

And they continued steadfastly in the apostles' doctrine and fellowship, in the breaking of bread, and in prayers. Then fear came upon every soul, and many wonders and signs were done through the apostles. Now all who believed were together, and had all things in common... So continuing daily with one accord in the temple, and breaking bread from house to house, they ate their food with gladness and simplicity of heart, praising God and having favor with all the people. And the Lord added to the church daily those who were being saved.

—Acts 2:42—44, 46–47

So there we have the basics. No committees or planning programmes are evident at all. There's ample evidence that nothing was done spontaneously but rather after much prayer and *only as God directed*. Those are important words.

The need to get back to basics in church arose during a discussion with some friends from our church. It was interesting how rapidly we went from open meetings for prayer, with the prayer itself setting the agenda, to talking about the requirements for a committee to identify what each person should bring to contribute to the accompanying supper. It seems that we are constitutionally unable to just leave the agenda in God's hands and rely upon the people to do whatever is necessary.

So what are the basics?

1. Community prayer centred on the Kingdom.
2. A community spirit of togetherness.
3. Total reliance upon God to set the agenda.
4. A focus on learning about Kingdom living.
5. No selfishness.

Applying the Fertilizer

I can't believe that I'm actually attempting to answer this one. This is where we get out of the theoretical realm and into the practical. So, practically speaking, we start the process by starting to live as described in the Sermon on the Mount. It's an attitudinal change, and it isn't something we can do on our own anyway. It may sound a little blasé to say, "It's the result of prayer," in actuality it's true. If we truly work at our citizen attitudes, we will change—and we might not even notice it. But others will.

Two very similar invitations are presented below. Do you notice the Acts difference?

We will meet again this coming Wednesday. I'll be continuing to lead from Mark. You are welcome to join us at my house as of 7:30 p.m. Feel free to bring a little snack to enjoy before we start with the topic at 8:15.

We will meet again this coming Wednesday at 7:30 p.m. so as to start with the topic at 8:00 p.m. to finish on time for prayer. Looking forward to seeing you and have a great weekend.

Prayer, desire, and obedience—as far as I can determine, that's all there is to it. No viable programmes or planned agenda will result in a vibrant New Testament church. There are no sermons the pastor can present, books we can read, or study material to provide the needed information. Speaking about a church, all that's required is for a group of believers to go before God in prayer and seek out His Kingdom—without preconditions. The precondition bit is the stumbling block for most of us. That, and our own impatience. From there on, we are in God's hands and you can be sure that He will take good care of us. We just have to follow His instructions, including the guide for living that can be found in Matthew's gospel.

That wasn't so bad, so let's consider the next question.

Identifying Marks

The first and most prevalent sign of a growing church is the manifested presence of the Holy Spirit. I'm not referring to speaking in tongues, although this may occur, but rather to the evidence of miracles, and of dreams or visions as well.

Let's talk about the latter first. It's not unlikely that a Muslim, living in an Islamic country, could live his life through without ever encountering a Christian. There just aren't that many of us living there. Yet Muslims are coming to know Christ in growing numbers. I've heard numerous stories of Muslims approaching Christians on the street, someone they don't even know, and asking them the way of salvation. When queried, the convert says words to the effect that God gave him a vision of the man he was to seek out.

With regards to miracles, these were the signs God used to prove that the early church was working with His blessing. Churches today often claim that the age of miracles ended with the disciples, but there are too many wonderful stories of healings and conversions to believe that. The dearth of miracles in this century is more due to lack of belief and a refusal to acknowledge the working of the Holy Spirit by Christians.

The same situation can be found in Matthew 13. Christ had returned to His own home but found himself powerless because of his neighbours' unbelief. The neighbours said,

"And His sisters, are they not all with us? Where then did this Man *get all these things?" So they were offended at Him.*
But Jesus said to them, "A prophet is not without honor except in his own country and in his own house."
Now He did not do many mighty works there because of their unbelief.

—Matthew 13:56–58 (emphasis added)

We are His church and part of His family. Isn't it sad that it can truly be said of us that He couldn't do many miracles among us because of our unbelief?

A growing church can be identified by the smiles on the faces of its members.

> *Then Philip went down to the city of Samaria and preached Christ to them. And the multitudes with one accord heeded the things spoken by Philip, hearing and seeing the miracles which he did. For unclean spirits, crying with a loud voice, came out of many who were possessed; and many who were paralyzed and lame were healed. And there was great joy in that city.*
>
> —Acts 8:5–8

> *So continuing daily with one accord in the temple, and breaking bread from house to house, they ate their food with gladness and simplicity of heart, praising God and having favor with all the people. And the Lord added to the church daily those who were being saved.*
>
> —Acts 2:46–47

A growing church can be identified by the eagerness of its members to meet and fellowship together.

Finally, a growing church can be identified by the eagerness of its members to learn more about Christ and His Kingdom.

Biblical proof for all of these points can be found in the book of Acts, particularly in the first six or seven chapters.

This has ended up being a lot longer than I had intended when I started. I do hope you've been able to stay with me all the way through, and I hope I have indeed given you something to think about!

Chapter 6

A Lot to Think About

CONSIDER THIS: YOU HAVE RECEIVED CERTAIN KNOWLEDGE THAT YOUR VERY best friend, your spouse, a brother, or someone else with whom you are extremely close is going to die next Monday morning. This dear friend is not a Christian. On Sunday, he/she is going to visit with you and will only stay for a couple of hours before you part company for the very last time. Where would you take them to meet Jesus?

Something to think about!

Chapter 7

Choosing the Right Church

THINKING ABOUT YOUR PERSONAL SITUATION ONLY, GIVEN THAT YOU WERE granted one chance to introduce a friend to God, would you take him/her to your church? Did you select your church because of its programming, music style, size, or on the basis of its gospel message? Strange as it may seem, a positive answer to the second question is not necessarily compatible with Scripture. As for the first question, you will have to read right through to the end of this chapter to find the answer.

When God dictated His message for the seven churches in Asia to John, He identified serious problems that He wanted corrected lest judgement fall upon them. One particular church and community, Thyatira, was given over to sexual immorality. A false prophetess had enticed the believers and many had followed her teaching. God pronounced judgement upon those who followed her, but for those who hadn't, He merely told them to hold firm to what they believed: at no point did He instruct them to leave the church. The church in Pergamos had allowed followers of the Nicolaitans and Balaam to become a part of the church, and they were chastised for it. They were told to clean up their act and get their church back on the right footing, or else God would do it for them. But those loyal to their faith were not told to leave.

Christianity is not an institution, nor is it a business. In fact, we might be better off if we dropped the term entirely. We are Christ-followers. So, what would Christ do if He were a member of a dysfunctional church?

Leadership

A sorry tale of poor church leadership can be traced throughout the gospel story of Jesus' life. Indeed, the church leadership provided Him with most of the material He needed for His lessons on Kingdom living. "Look at the church leadership," He would thunder, "and then do the opposite."

The scribes and Pharisees are the focus of much of His most colourful language. He calls them every name under the sun, but He never tells the people to get out of the synagogue and start their own services. To the contrary, Scripture tells us that He went out of His way to ensure that He attended services Himself in whatever town He was in on that particular Sabbath. And not only did He attend, but He participated, regardless of whether they sang hymns or psalms or just choruses.

As He left for Heaven after His resurrection, He gave one final bit of instruction to His followers: "Go and teach the lessons I taught you." The wording is important. He didn't tell His followers to go and start a new church, but rather He ordered them to follow His example and teach as He had taught.

In the Acts, we find that this is exactly what the church did.

And daily in the temple, and in every house, they did not cease teaching and preaching Jesus as the Christ.

—Acts 5:42

It's more likely that the shift in meeting places occurred through the church authorities refusing the use of the facilities than from the church leaving the temple or synagogue.

Charles Wesley and Martin Luther sought reform within their respective churches and both were eventually forced by their church leadership to take their ideas elsewhere.

You Are the Light

So what has this to do with selecting the correct church? If you're just moving into the neighbourhood, the answer is that it has nothing to do with it at all. But if you are currently involved with a local church, the answer is far more complicated.

John's comments to the seven churches in Asia suggest that people should stay with the church they are at. Indeed, those in Pergamos were held partially responsible for the condition their church was in and told in no uncertain terms to do something about it. In the Sermon on the Mount, Christ compares citizens of Heaven to lights. So think of each church as being a single string of Christmas lights, with each believer in that church being one of the bulb and socket assemblies. If one bulb is removed, there's a gap in the lighting that can be more noticeable because of its absence than the remainder of the illuminated bulbs. God has positioned each of us within His body in the exact place He wants us. Together we provide the light that directs others to Him. If we choose to go elsewhere, we leave a dark spot on the path that could cause someone else to stumble.

If we are in the place God wants us, we don't need to worry about poor doctrine or shoddy teaching bringing us down. 2 Peter 2:9 gives us total assurance of this:

...then the Lord knows how to deliver the godly out of temptations and to reserve the unjust under punishment for the day of judgment...

I have only quoted the one verse, but you will find the full passage quite instructional.

Poor doctrine isn't the usual reason for people changing churches. Instead it is usually programming or personality conflict. Every pastor I've ever met would be ecstatic if his church was able to provide programming for every age group. Sadly, the lack of willing workers means that he generally has to pick and choose which programme(s) to support. So if the church down the street offers a Saturday workshop for men and I want a programme offering a Saturday workshop, I'll start attending the church down the street rather than going to the pastor and volunteering to start a Saturday workshop for men. It's easier to change churches than it is to volunteer to fill a need.

Remember that string of Christmas lights? If Satan succeeds in separating a believer from God's chosen position, that believer will suffer. True, the church's testimony is diminished, but the transposed believer doesn't fit in anywhere else. It isn't possible to simply take the bulb out and put it elsewhere. The rest of the light strings are already complete, so the transposed bulb sits idly by, unused and useless until it is either broken or lost.

Simply put, we should let God choose our house of worship. Let's get back to the question that started this whole thing. Where should I take a person to meet Christ? How about my own living room? If they don't see Christ in me, it isn't likely that any conference or crusade I introduce them to will have any greater success.

Something to think about!

Chapter 8

Lead Us Not

Let no one say when he is tempted, "I am tempted by God"; for God cannot be tempted by evil, nor does He Himself tempt anyone."
—James 1:13

And lead us not into temptation, but deliver us from evil: For thine is the kingdom, and the power, and the glory, for ever. Amen.
—Matthew 6:13, KJV

EVERY TIME I THINK I KNOW WHAT A VERSE IS SAYING, I END UP PROVING myself wrong. Every time I read a passage, even a well-known passage, with the intent to discover what God is saying to me, I uncover a new (to me) truth.

Reading Matthew 6:13 was no exception. Earlier in His sample prayer, Jesus prayed that the will of the Father would take precedence. Now He comes back to this concept with regards to temptation.

As is evident from the James 1:13 passage, God does not tempt. Therefore scholars and teachers have rightfully ruled out the notion that Jesus is complicit in our temptations.

To begin to understand this verse is to begin to understand both the interaction of God with man in spite of his sinful condition, and the need for such interaction to counteract the otherwise overwhelming power of Satan. Let me try to explain.

Satan rules this earth at the moment. Five minutes listening to the news should be enough to convince anyone but the most ardent atheist that this is the case. Satan, however, is limited to being in only one place at a time. Rather than having to lie in wait for each individual, he relies upon snares and pitfalls and baits them carefully with attractive items that will catch the attention of his intended victims. Temptation is always appealing; that's why it is called temptation. The things that tempt us aren't always bad things either. Taking your son to the ball game is a good thing. Calling in sick to take your son to the game is not so good. Temptation affects our vocabulary. We rationalize rather than lie, and borrow rather than steal. But enough of that for the moment. We'll come back to temptation a little later.

I have discovered so much whilst studying this verse that I hardly know how to begin. The lessons start with the very first phrase. "Lead us not" implies that we are allowing Him to lead, and that can be a problem when we try to align our prayer life with our actions. The normal approach, unfortunately, more resembles Russian roulette. The prayer goes something like this: "Lord, show me the direction you want me to go." But the action is more like: "I want to do this, and if it isn't right I'm sure that God will let me know." Getting an answer to prayer often requires patience. If we have asked Him to lead, we really should wait for Him to step out before we begin to move.

There is a castle in Scotland located upon an island in the middle of a bog lake. Today a bridge links castle and mainland, but during medieval times visitors to the castle were blindfolded and led by experienced guides along the underwater paving stones that led to the castle. The path twisted and turned back on itself several times, and the unwary, unprepared, first-time or unwanted guest who attempted to find his own way would soon find himself stuck in the mud and unable to proceed either forward or backward: easy pickings for the castle defenders during times of war.

Remember the instructions Paul gave to the Ephesians regarding preparation?

Wherefore take unto you the whole armour of God, that ye may be able to withstand in the evil day, and having done all, to stand.
—Ephesians 6:13, KJV (emphasis added)

When you are ready and prepared, stand still and wait for orders. Jesus is a leader who leads from the front.

> *And I saw heaven opened, and behold a white horse; and he that sat upon him was called Faithful and True, and in righteousness he doth judge and make war. His eyes were as a flame of fire, and on his head were many crowns; and he had a name written, that no man knew, but he himself. And he was clothed with a vesture dipped in blood: and his name is called The Word of God. And the armies which were in heaven followed him upon white horses, clothed in fine linen, white and clean.*
>
> —Revelation 19:11–14, KJV

Remember the words He used when He called His disciples? "Follow me and I will make you..." Want more examples?

> *Not according to the covenant that I made with their fathers in the day when I took them by the hand to lead them out of the land of Egypt; because they continued not in my covenant, and I regarded them not, saith the Lord.*
>
> —Hebrews 8:9, KJV

> *For the Lamb which is in the midst of the throne shall feed them, and shall lead them unto living fountains of waters: and God shall wipe away all tears from their eyes.*
>
> —Revelation 7:17, KJV

> *They shall come with weeping, and with supplications will I lead them: I will cause them to walk by the rivers of waters in a straight way, wherein they shall not stumble: for I am a father to Israel...*
>
> —Jeremiah 31:9, KJV

> *To him the porter openeth; and the sheep hear his voice: and he calleth his own sheep by name, and leadeth them out.*
>
> —John 10:3, KJV

The opening salutation in the Lord's prayer is "Our Father," Remembering that, re-read the promise in Jeremiah 31:9. The consequences of not following are illustrated in Hebrews 8:9; indeed, the entire history of the Jewish people is a tragic illustration of a people who tried to go it alone.

Satan has the authority to set traps, but he isn't allowed to use abnormal events. Jesus promises that there will be a way out. But just as with the path to the castle on the island, you will need a guide.

> *There hath no temptation taken you but such as is common to man: but God is faithful, who will not suffer you to be tempted above that ye are able; but will with the temptation also make a way to escape, that ye may be able to bear it.*
>
> —1 Corinthians 10:13, KJV

Satan sometimes uses our service for God in his tempting. Peter tried to walk on water, and for a few steps he was successful. Then he took his eyes off Jesus and began to sink. Did he become afraid, as is generally thought, or was he tempted by the glory of his own accomplishments? With what we know about his personality, it wouldn't be wrong to suggest that he started to gloat inwardly: *Look at me, you eleven in the boat. I'm walking on water! None of you had the nerve to get out, only me. I'm ready to follow Jesus anywhere but you aren't.* Possible, isn't it? And then came that sinking feeling.

Prayer is answered when we keep our eyes on Jesus and follow in His footsteps. Satan's snares are only successful when we try to make our own way.

"But deliver us from evil" is more accurately translated as "but deliver us from the evil one." When Jesus was teaching us to pray, He was well aware that we would unfortunately take our eyes off Him just as Peter did, especially during times when we should be rejoicing in God because of victories won or something worthwhile accomplished.

Human nature insists on taking credit for accomplishments, but the Kingdom way is to give the credit to God and then rejoice. That doesn't mean that we can't be happy about what we have achieved. Indeed, God is always ready to congratulate His followers. Those words—

"Well done, thou good and faithful servant" (Matthew 25:21, KJV)—are applicable to us as well. The hard thing is remembering that if it weren't for God's gifts, the accomplishment wouldn't be possible.

But I digress. There will be times when our paths take us perilously close to Satan. At no time are we strong enough to take him on. Mountaintop experiences in our Christian walk are really great. They occur only after a lot of struggle, and the view from the top is spectacular. They only have one major disadvantage: you can't stay there—and the only way to the next peak is to descend into the valley between. Having reached the top, we are certain that we have it made. From one peak, we can see all the way to the next one, and with what we have already endured, it doesn't look that hard. Split churches, the Christian divorce rate, and ministers caught up in adultery, greed, and pride are proof enough that taking the first step towards the next peak before Jesus shows us the way down is a sure way to end up stuck in the mud.

Following Jesus is not an abstract thought but a practical solution for today's problems. There are enough illustrations in the New Testament identifying how Christ thought and acted in a variety of circumstances that it's possible to pattern our own lives after Him. He wants us to follow Him, but not blindly or without thinking things through. That would make us robots, the antithesis of God's purpose in our creation. You do realise that God created us with the ability to make bad choices and then sacrificed His son in order that we could escape the consequences of that bad choice, right?

What happens when there are two or three choices, all appearing to be good? Prayer is our connection to God. Simply put, it is nothing more than a conversation. Awesome! We can talk to the Ruler of the Universe, and He will answer, for that is the purpose of prayer. Each of the verses we have reviewed implies the need for a response, and God promises that He will answer. Awesome! Prayer is the bridge that enables us to become citizens of the Kingdom whilst still living here on earth.

Something to think about!

Chapter 9

All or Nothing

FROM TIME TO TIME THROUGHOUT THESE PAGES, I WILL DIVERT FROM THE normal format and include little bits of scientific information that points to the efficacy of the creation story—or conversely, to the failings of evolution. I am not a scientist, nor do I have any scientific credentials.

The information I relay can all be found in the public domain, so why do I consider it important enough to spend time researching these issues or to ensure that you are aware of them? As part of my work in Europe, I was required to read and comment on numerous research articles involving both equipment and procedures development. Normally, by the time I finished the executive summary I would have already formed an opinion as to the accuracy or applicability of the document in question. Sadly, I seldom had occasion to change that first impression. Most people, I think you will agree, have a similar reaction to documents, letters, and newspapers.

The Bible is considered to be the story of God's dealings with man. Consider then that you are picking up the Bible for the very first time. As with most books, you turn to page one and read the first paragraph. And the first sentence of the first paragraph reads: "In the beginning God created..." Is it fact or fiction? If you don't believe the first page, as written, what are the chances that you are going to accept the rest of it? If Page 1 (the story of creation in seven days) contains inaccuracies, then it's logical to assume that Page 794 (Romans 3) or Page 797 (Romans 6) contains inaccuracies as well. Conversely, if we can support Page 1 with scientific or logical evidence, the content of the other pages is more likely to be accepted as true. And so, I write.

It's Logical

Do you believe that the Bible is God's testimony to us and was composed by Him? I suspect all of you will say yes. You will quote 2 Timothy 3:15—*"All scripture is given by inspiration of God"* (KJV)—as proof, and will be absolutely correct. So how many of you will stake your testimony on the following: that God created the Heavens and the Earth, and that He did it in six days?

Today's news is chock full of reports from governments approving homosexual marriages, abortion, euthanasia, assisted suicide, and other issues that are antithetical to what we believe. In almost all of these cases, the church is practically invisible. When a minister or theologian does take a biblical stance, he is inevitably ridiculed by the press, or in some cases even charged with a violation of a human rights code. At the very least he is branded as a bigot, a Neanderthal, or as seems to be the ultimate insult these days, an evangelical.

The church as a whole generally remains silent, much as Peter did in the court of the High Priest during Christ's trial. When confronted, the church denies the laws of God by extemporising—again, the same as Peter. It has approached too close to the warmth of the so-deemed scientific fire. It's true that some denominational organisations or portions thereof will speak out, but the press can always locate some minister who will come out in support of the liberalisation and paint his fellow pastor as being out of touch with the new reality.

Not good, is it? But what can we, as individuals, do about it? Fighting all these issues is both costly and, in the end, futile. It's like playing whack-a-mole. Swing at one evil and a dozen others will take its place. Whilst it is essential that we establish and maintain a consistent stance regarding all these issues—hard enough in itself—going to war against them is a battle we cannot win.

Less than fifty years ago, the laws in all our nations were based upon biblical principles. Our moral code was firmly positioned on the same code that Moses recorded five thousand years ago. Fifty years ago, the vast majority of our nations' population would have answered "Yes" to the first question in this chapter. Today, the answer would be "No." The reason for this is found in the response that those same people of fifty years ago would have given to the second question. When you don't believe in Genesis, it isn't long before you have doubts about the rest. And logically speaking, you are absolutely correct. If I didn't believe Genesis, I wouldn't be attending church or writing this book.

As Christians when testifying to others, we use the information found in the four gospels. Occasionally we quote one or two of the psalms or the letters of Paul. We seldom refer to Genesis. Why is that?

In 1 Corinthians 1:22–23, we read,

For Jews request a sign, and Greeks seek after wisdom; but we preach Christ crucified, to the Jews a stumbling block and to the Greeks foolishness...

Why was a crucified Christ only a stumbling block to the Jews but utter foolishness to the Greeks? It was because the Jews already had a basis of knowledge regarding Christ; they had been taught about the Messiah for centuries, and knowledge of the Father had been instilled in them. They believed it. But the Greeks were pantheistic. They believed in a multitude of rather immature, self-centred, and immoral gods, so the concept of a single God who had a standard of moral absolutes and cared enough to die for them was totally alien. They just didn't understand. In order to reach them, Paul had to start with the basics and teach them about God. We see this in Acts 14 and Acts 17. In both lessons, Paul started with the creation because this is our foundation. This is where it all started.

People today are like those Greeks. When we witness, we are witnessing from a position totally foreign to most listeners. Biblical principles are no longer taught in school or followed in the courts. People don't believe that the Bible is the Word, and that is because we ourselves deny its authenticity. We don't understand, and so we avoid Genesis: the book of beginnings. This lack of understanding is a relatively new phenomenon. At any rate, there was no confusion in the minds of the writers of Scripture. Genesis is referred to regularly throughout the New Testament.

When people make statements that imply that evolution is a science, and that creation is a myth or bad science, we don't know how to respond. In truth, neither is science, and both are beliefs. I repeat that neither creation nor evolution meets the strict criteria for science, in that they are neither observable nor repeatable. The facts are mineralised bits of skeleton found today and not observed in their natural environment. In one, we have written our own theory and now are trying to fit the evidence to it whilst in the other we are examining the evidence and seeing how it fits the story we have been given. Once you accept that as a starting point, the proofs for creation are self-evident, as are the failings of evolution. There are loads of books, magazines, and websites that provide the scientifically proven evidence supporting creation. We just have to look for them.

But we have to start with Genesis, just as Paul did with the Greeks, and we have to support our testimony with facts. Peter foretold the hold that evolution would have on society in his second letter:

> *...knowing this first: that scoffers will come in the last days, walking according to their own lusts, and saying, "Where is the promise of His coming? For since the fathers fell asleep, all things continue as they were from the beginning of creation." For* this they willfully forget*: that by the word of God the heavens were of old, and the earth standing out of water and in the water, by which the world that then existed perished, being flooded with water.*
>
> —2 Peter 3:3–6 (emphasis added)

It is also something that we wilfully forget.

It's not something that the humanists forget, though. Not even for a minute. In fact, it's one of their operating rules. They constantly aim their salvos at the foundation of our faith: Genesis.

The humanists have declared their belief that the universe is self-existing, that it was not created, and that man is simply part of nature, having emerged as the result of a natural process. They believe that everything having to do with man starts with man, and never with God. From a description of their plan of attack:

I am convinced that the battle for humankind's future must be waged and won in the public school classroom by teachers who correctly perceive their role as the proselytizers of a new faith: a religion of humanity that recognizes and respects the spark of what theologians call divinity in every human being. These teachers must embody the same selfless dedication as the most rabid fundamentalist preachers... to convey humanist values in whatever subject they teach, regardless of the educational level.[1]

They start by denying the truth of Genesis, and when we respond with "Jesus loves you," well, we aren't even in the same battle. How then should we respond to the prevailing notions on abortion, homosexuality, and other attacks on our core values? We should do so as Jesus did when confronted with a question on marriage. He went straight back to Genesis and the creation of Adam and Eve. So should we.

The Bible says, "In the beginning, God..."

Something to think about!

---

1 John J. Dumphy, "A Religion for a New Age," *The Humanist*, January–February (1983), 26.

Chapter 10

Adjusting the Facts to Fit the Question

IT SNOWED HERE LAST WEEKEND. IN THE MIDDLE OF IT, SANDY AND I decided that we needed a taste of spring and new growth, so we ventured down the highway and eventually ended up at the botanical gardens. Just what the doctor ordered! Plants, warmth, blossoms, and even a few tropical creatures.

Meet the golden dart frog. Look, but don't touch—at least not a wild one. A kiss between the princess and this particular frog prince could be fatal. A golden dart frog packs enough venom into his two-inch (five-centimetre) frame to kill ten grown men. The Emberá people of Colombia tipped their blowgun darts with the venom to ensure their kill when hunting, hence the species' name. The poison is a neurotoxin, which, as its name implies, attacks the nervous system. The resulting electrical depolarization results in cardiac arrhythmia and death.[2]

Herpetologists (the official job title for a frog scientist) have been unable to identify any glands or organs within the frog that actually manufacture the poison. (The golden dart frogs that are bred and raised in laboratories are not poisonous.) The primary diet of a dart frog in his home environment consists of ants plus spiders, termites, beetles, millipedes, and flies—anything that wanders past. They aren't particular, but ants are the most common. Ants and certain other insects contain alkaloids (the base chemical for several poisons), but at nowhere near the level of concentration found in the golden dart frog,

---

2 For those interested, details can be found at http://www.newworldencyclopedia.org/entry/Poison_dart_frog

leading scientists to believe that whilst the frog lacks the ability to produce a toxin, it appears to be able to chemically modify the amino acids contained in its primary food source to produce the far more deadly poison. It works fast, too. If a predator were to eat a golden dart frog, it would be feeling sick before it was able to swallow, and it would certainly not live long enough to consume a second frog for desert.

When a dart frog is taken from its home environment and fed a diet of fruit flies and crickets, it will lose its toxicity. Given the choice in captivity, dart frogs won't even eat ants, preferring other delicacies, despite the fact that ants are its dominant food form in the wild. Scientists think that the alkaloids leave a bitter taste.

There are a number of different species of dart frog, some more deadly than others. They are distinguished by colour and habitat with the more brilliant generally, but not always, being the most toxic. It is believed by frog scientists, but not proven, that the bright colours serve as a warning to predators so they won't inadvertently pick the wrong frog in the pond and die.

Dart frogs provide a unique challenge for scientists, for some of the species can only be traced back approximately six thousand years, and that is only yesterday for an evolutionist. If the earth and its creatures are millions of years old, how on earth did a bright yellow frog survive up until six thousand years ago with no defence mechanism? After all these millions of years, what was the advantage gained by the frog by suddenly becoming yellow?

Scripture has no problem with a six-thousand-year timeframe at all. In fact, it ties in fairly closely with the biblical time line. Prior to man's sin and eviction from the garden, there was no death. Consequently, a pretty yellow frog had no need to process and store up a neurotoxin. Its own diet would have consisted of something other than insects: perhaps seeds or water plants of some nature. For the dart frog, banishment from Eden brought about both a change in diet (to ants, spiders, and other insects) and a very potent and needed defence mechanism. God probably built in the capability way back during creation week; there was no requirement for anything to evolve.

Here are some more questions that science has been unable to resolve, yet require answers if an evolutionary pathway is to be followed:

1. Given that dart frogs' diet of choice doesn't include ants, how did dart frogs learn to eat them in sufficient quantities and over a long enough period to first develop the ability to store toxins and develop the glands required to secrete it?

2. How did a yellow frog survive long enough to develop its poison defence mechanism?

3. Snakes are a frog's greatest enemy. Snakes generally never make contact with their young. They certainly don't conduct classes in diet. They lay eggs and leave them. Given that any snake that consumes a dart frog dies, how did a snake pass on the information to avoid eating a golden frog?

4. The dart frog has one enemy other than man: a particular variety of snake. How did this one snake develop the ability to neutralise the poison?

5. Given the obvious advantage that the poison provides and given the supposed millions of years available for development, why aren't dart frogs the most common frog on the planet?

6. Why does the evolutionary timeline seem to begin only six thousand years ago?

7. How did a yellow frog survive before that time? Conversely, why did a green (or some other colour) frog wait so long to change colours, and what was the advantage to the frog of doing so?

8. Creationists believe that God created all things and simultaneously established the pecking order between different species. Without God's programming of the minds of predators to avoid yellow frogs, how is it possible that a bird that feeds on frogs was able to pass on the knowledge of the fatal consequences of eating one particular species of frog when contact with that frog causes almost immediate death?

These are basic questions without satisfactory answers. It is more logical to believe that God created and that it was good. With that as a starting point, the answers become self-evident. Join with the psalmist: all creation displays His handiwork—and that is something to think about!

Chapter 11

Learning from Nature

I FOUND THE DART FROG SO FASCINATING THAT I DECIDED TO CONTINUE HIS story. With the last chapter as an introduction, we shall see just where my mind's encounter with this little creature has led me.3

Ministers regularly regale us with stories of what might have been if only the serpent hadn't been so persuasive. Man's disobedience definitely resulted in his life taking a decided turn for the worst. Simultaneously, that same sin had a catastrophic effect on the living habits of every single breathing creature. The prophet Isaiah, in his description of life in that future era when Christ establishes His millennial reign here on earth, was also describing life in the Garden of Eden.

> *The wolf also shall dwell with the lamb, the leopard shall lie down with the young goat, the calf and the young lion and the fatling together; and a little child shall lead them. The cow and the bear shall graze; their young ones shall lie down together; and the lion shall eat straw like the ox. The nursing child shall play by the cobra's hole, and the weaned child shall put his hand in the viper's den.*
>
> —Isaiah 11:6–8

No animal was left unaffected by Adam's sin. At the same time Adam was learning to sew fig leaves together, an emerald tree boa was

---

3 Strictly for the purpose of this illustration, I assume that God created the golden dart frog within the first six days, and that it was one of the creatures named by Adam in the Garden. It is also possible that this frog shares ancestry with all other frogs as part of the frog "kind" as described in Genesis. No one knows.

starting to swallow his very first (and possibly last) golden dart frog. Think about it: far from the concept of gradual changes over a prolonged period of time, in actuality the diet of every animal changed overnight. Neo-predators learnt to stalk, run down, bite, squeeze, or spear other animals. Their erstwhile prey learnt to listen intently for the sound of wings, watch for shadows, and carefully sniff the air for the scent of wolves, lions, or bears. Frogs started snapping flies out of the air with their tongues, or scooping up ants as they emerged from their holes. Every living creature became dinner for another, and many fought amongst themselves to protect food sources, juveniles, and mates, as they too were evicted from the garden.

Did God initiate physical changes to animals to develop the various attack, defence, or avoidance mechanisms seen in all animals today after the fall, or were the latent tendencies always there? Palaeontology cannot answer that question. No one knows how quickly these changes occurred, but the habits of animals today assure us that change indeed occurred, whilst Isaiah 11 tells us that God's plan never included death.

With reference to the dart frog, what we know is that approximately six thousand years ago a little yellow frog started eating ants. Some of his brothers and sisters preferred the taste of flies and moths, as they weren't as bitter, but unfortunately these yellow frogs soon vanished: devoured by the birds, snakes, and lizards that had discovered the wonders of fresh-caught frog. But this one little fellow and his family had grown accustomed to the taste of ants, and they ate them almost exclusively.

Now, it wasn't long before all the birds, snakes (except one), and lizards that had discovered the wonders of fresh-caught frog crossed the little yellow frogs off their dinner menu, as touching its skin had become almost instantaneously fatal. With only a single enemy, one would think that golden dart frogs would rule the pond, yet that isn't the case: one enemy unaffected by the defence is sufficient to ensure caution. The dart frog still had to be wary of all snakes, since it never knew which one was lurking in ambush.

One of Satan's favourite tactics is to attach different names to things, thus lessening their significance in our minds. The very first sin ever committed is a case in point. How often do we jokingly blame Eve for our fallen condition, saying that she ate the apple first? We say, "Adam only took a bite because she had him wrapped around her little finger." Or we use some other derogatory comment to cast the blame upon the other sex. She didn't make Adam follow her example. Adam and Eve didn't bite into an apple; they ate of the fruit of the tree of the knowledge of good and evil! It gave us the capability of distinguishing right from wrong, but that ability didn't come with the necessary skills required to shun all evil. We all have our favourite sin.

So what, you may ask, could all this possibly have to do with a frog? The first golden dart frog either had the latent capability to defend himself through poison even though, until his diet changed, he was harmless to touch, or even (yes, princess) to kiss, or it was given the defence by the creator as it was leaving the garden. Once it started eating ants and other insects with a high alkaloid level, those hitherto unused glands started to exude a highly concentrated neurotoxin that provided the previously helpless frog with an impenetrable defensive shield against all would-be predators, except of course that one lowly snake.

Just like that very first frog, all men and women are born fully equipped with the latent capability to distinguish evil. Adam's sin gave us that ability. But it isn't enough to know the difference if that knowledge doesn't stop us from doing it anyway. The temptation to sin comes at us from all directions, and Satan will certainly identify our own particular weakness and focus his efforts on it. We will sin.

When an individual becomes a Christian, he experiences a number of changes, but one in particular stands out: for the first time in his life, the new Christian is endowed with an external power to aid him in resisting the temptation to "do it" one more time. Instead of having to go it alone, he has the Holy Spirit within him to help to say "No" in just the same way as our domestically raised frog has within him the latent ability to process and store poison.

As you may recall, the internal processes possessed by the dart frog cannot actually manufacture the ingredients that make up the neurotoxin with which it defends itself. The base ingredients are obtained through diet. In the same manner, a Christian's ability to choose comes as a direct result of changes in his spiritual diet. Our choice of friends, movies, television programmes, books, and especially time spent in Bible study and prayer are all protein-enriched activities for the mind.

What makes up a healthy spiritual diet? That's an excellent question for another day. Suffice it for now to consider the words of David in Psalm 1.

> *Blessed is the man Who walks not in the counsel of the ungodly, nor stands in the path of sinners, nor sits in the seat of the scornful;* but his delight is in the law *of the Lord, and in His law* he meditates day and night. *He shall be like a tree planted by the rivers of water, that brings forth its fruit in its season, whose leaf also shall not wither; and whatever he does shall prosper.*
>
> —Psalm 1:1–3 (emphasis added)

In just a few short verses, David provides a succinct yet comprehensive list of both beneficial and detrimental activities, guaranteeing success to all those who follow his advice.

When dart frogs are captured in the wild and fed a different diet, they eventually lose their toxicity and can be handled freely and even fed to predators. They become harmless, but even worse, they become vulnerable.

So it is with Christians. "We are what we eat" is as true in the spiritual world as it is in the physical. In Hebrews 5, the apostle tries to describe the priesthood of Christ to the early Jewish church. Partway through his writing, the author suddenly seems to throw up his hands in despair and lashes out at the church and its total lack of growth. "Instead of becoming teachers of the word," he says, "you still need nursing. You haven't grown enough to be able to identify with what is right." Notice what he has to say about diet:

> *Concerning him we have much to say, and it is hard to explain, since you have become dull of hearing. For though by this time you ought to be teachers, you have need again for someone to teach you the elementary principles of the oracles of God, and you have come to need*

milk and not solid food. For everyone who partakes only of milk is not accustomed to the word of righteousness, for he is an infant. But solid food is for the mature, who because of practice have their senses trained to discern good and evil.

—Hebrews 5:10–14, NASB

If you don't eat the right food, you can't develop a shield against evil. Remember the parable of the sower and the seed? The seed that fell on stony soil germinated quickly, but its root system was unable to penetrate far enough into the soil to draw out the necessary nutrients. And so it died.

Now take special note of what Isaiah has to say:

Ho! Everyone who thirsts, come to the waters; and you who have no money, come, buy and eat. Yes, come, buy wine and milk without money and without price. Why do you spend money for what is not bread, and your wages for what does not satisfy? Listen carefully to Me, and eat what is good, and let your soul delight itself in abundance.

Incline your ear, and come to Me. Hear, and your soul shall live; and I will make an everlasting covenant with you.

—Isaiah 55:1–3

The dart frog without the proper diet has no defence against predators. Christians without the proper diet have no defence against predators. What's for supper?

Something to think about!

Chapter 12

God Doing His Thing

"GOD KEEPS DOING HIS THING" IS ONE OF THE LINES I LIVE BY. I SAY IT when I realize I've stumbled into the centre of something far bigger than myself.

A student leader at the university in Brussels asked if I would conduct a weekly Bible study on campus. One evening, our normal meeting room was full of people, so we looked around for one that was less popular. The one we ended up in had only one person doing his dishes. It took him two hours to finish up, and now he will be attending the group weekly. God was doing His thing! Just like the times I've found myself preparing a short note for these ramblings and ended up writing on issues I had never before thought about or cared about. A reader has replied with a kind note mentioning that this thought has helped with a decision they had to make. In times when the right words come to me in a conversation—answers to tough issues, clear explanations of the Gospel, words from God for people—it's God doing His thing.

Evangelism, discipleship, and the church are God's thing, not ours. He invites us, calls us, and gifts us to be a part of it, but the bottom line is God, not us. Two basic truths accompany this concept.

First, if this is God's thing, God is responsible for carrying it out. Every week in home group and in church, we need to remember this simple truth and rely upon it. God should be part of the preparation and presentation of every devotional, every sermon, and every worship service. Right? No! God should be the leader! I have to believe that God is preparing each participant's heart, providing the words and then the follow-up Spirit-leading each and every week.

I am not claiming that God supplies every word I write or that is spoken at home group. I wish I could make that claim, but the fact remains that most words spoken are a result of the speaker's preconceived thoughts. Otherwise, we would have perfect agreement regarding doctrine, and we know that isn't true. My claim is that God will use each word spoken, even when in error, to accomplish His goal. Knowing that ministry is God's thing takes the pressure off of us; He is ultimately responsible for its fulfilment.

The second truth is a little harder to swallow. If this is God's thing, He gets the glory, not us.

When King Nebuchadnezzar gloated over Babylon, saying, *"Is not this great Babylon, that I have built... by my mighty power for the honor of my majesty?"* (Daniel 4:30), God stripped his glory, authority, and identity until he acknowledged that this was God's Kingdom, not his.

We easily get caught up in Kingdom-building—our church, our ministry, and our programme. We tighten our grip on our roles, vision, and ultimately our glory. When it's God's thing, programmes and roles are subject to His vision. His scope in any given situation, location, or individual is often far broader than we'll ever see. It is His Kingdom we are building, and it's for His glory.

So what is our role in this Kingdom which is out of our hands and beyond our scope? Faithfulness! God invites us, calls us, and gifts us to be part of building His Kingdom. We are not responsible for the whole thing, but we are responsible for the part God has entrusted to us.

Thus, the first challenge is to discover our role. Paul challenges Timothy to *"fan into flame the gift of God"* (2 Timothy 1:6, NIV) and to be faithful in carrying out His calling.

The second is to be faithful in that calling. I have heard it said that the blood of the martyrs is the seed of the church. Those martyrs saw none of the fruit of their work, but it is upon their faithful blood that we build the church today.

Something to think about!

Chapter 13

Meeting God

A REGULARLY QUOTED—AND OFTEN MISQUOTED—VERSE IS MATTHEW 7:7. Ask, seek, knock... remember it? Jesus is talking to the folks who have been following Him all around Galilee and explaining the Kingdom to them: that was His principal message. Matthew 4:17 says, *"From that time Jesus began to preach and to say, "Repent, for the kingdom of heaven is at hand."* The Kingdom is now. So Jesus is advertising the availability and the proximity of God's Kingdom. In this context, He presents the lessons in the Sermon on the Mount.

I stated at the start that this verse is often misquoted. I make this statement in the context of receiving things from God. This verse isn't about asking for and receiving things but about finding and entering the Kingdom of Heaven, which is what the Sermon on the Mount is all about. Instead, this verse implies that God will reveal Himself to anyone who honestly looks for Him. This promise isn't dependent upon the geographical location of the seeker, the era in which he lives, the presence of an evangelical missionary, or the availability of a copy of Scripture, although God may use any or all of these. Rather it is a promise of Christ Himself. The story of Nebuchadnezzar is proof of this.

As tyrants go, Nebuchadnezzar wasn't a bad guy. True, when he conquered Jerusalem he put many of its most prominent citizens to death, but he was also wise enough to assimilate the best of the captives he took in battle and incorporate them into his government. He was also religious. He knew there were gods and he sought to please them. The adventure that the three Hebrews had with the furnace was a result of him trying to encourage his people to worship one god that he had set up in the Grand Place. I guess his heart was in the right place, but he certainly wasn't a believer in religious freedom of choice. None of the translations I have available indicate that this was an image of himself, by the way. I even checked the Jewish version. We don't know who this image represented, but it is an error to imply that he was establishing himself as a god.

His first encounter with the true God was through the interpretation of a dream Daniel supplied. Nebuchadnezzar acknowledged that Daniel's God was the wisest one. He wasn't yet ready to add him to the pantheon of Babylonian gods, though.

Then came the furnace episode, and Nebuchadnezzar came to the conclusion that this God needed to be praised. He lined himself up as God's defender. You see, Nebuchadnezzar made the same mistake many of us do, thinking that God is somehow weak and needs man's help (Daniel 3:29). Nebuchadnezzar was a true New Age person (a little god).

Then came the second dream! Before we talk about that, though, I'll summarize what we know to this point. Nebuchadnezzar knew that the Hebrew God was wise (the first dream), and that this God was worthy of praise (furnace episode). But God wasn't personal to him yet. God was a spirit—a concept, but not a reality.

Now we come to the dream. Daniel interpreted the dream. He told Nebuchadnezzar that for seven years he was going to live in the fields like an animal. While this was happening, God would protect him, and at the end of this time he would know who was in charge. But there was a chance that it could be avoided if he acknowledged God's supremacy.

Nothing happened for about a year, and I guess Nebuchadnezzar probably forgot all about the dream. At any rate, he didn't change his habits any. Then it all happened just as the dream foretold, with one magnificent addition: God spoke.

Our friend the king was out in the garden, admiring all that he had accomplished and patting himself on the back. "Oh, what a great king I am. My, but I do good work. This place couldn't get along without me." These words weren't even completely out of his mouth when the voice of God spoke from Heaven, literally from the air around him. God spoke directly to him before he entered the state of madness and reminded him what was about to happen and why! As foretold, seven years later Nebuchadnezzar recovered and made this royal decree:

> ...*my understanding returned to me; and I blessed the Most High and praised and honored Him who lives forever: for His dominion is an everlasting dominion, and His kingdom is from generation to generation... Now I, Nebuchadnezzar, praise and extol and honor the King of heaven, all of whose works are truth, and His ways justice. And those who walk in pride He is able to put down.*
>
> —Daniel 4:34, 37

This is as clear a statement acknowledging God as any I have heard at any testimonial or baptismal service. Nebuchadnezzar believed! Daniel doesn't give any indication that anyone else followed in Nebuchadnezzar's footsteps. Indeed, his son Belshazzar lost his kingdom because he blasphemed God by using the temple treasures for a pagan celebration. The only explanation that fits is that Nebuchadnezzar believed in God and was open to finding Him personally. God honoured that belief and revealed Himself to him. The message of Nebuchadnezzar confesses that God's Kingdom is now.

It is time to go back to the beginning of this chapter. The message of Matthew 7 is this: if you look for Heaven, you will find it; if you ask for directions, they will be provided; and when you find Heaven and knock on the door, God Himself will open it up and invite you to come in. Oh, and you don't have wait until you die to belong. Matthew 7:8 assures us of this: *"For everyone who asks receives."*

And that is something to think about!

Chapter 14

Loving God

Then one of them, a lawyer, asked Him a question, testing Him, and saying, "Teacher, which is the great commandment in the law?"

Jesus said to him, "'You shall love the Lord your God with all your heart, with all your soul, and with all your mind.' This is the first and great commandment."

—Matthew 22:35–38

Oh how I love Jesus
Oh how I love Jesus
Oh how I love Jesus
Because He first loved me.

—Frederick Whitfield, 1855

LOVING GOD IS A TOPIC THAT SEEMS TO COME UP TIME AND AGAIN IN different forms, and this is as it should be, for our love relationship with God is pivotal to our salvation. Unfortunately, it seems that this love is part of a Rip Van Winkle world: it's there, but it's in extended hibernation and will not be aroused until we die and meet Him in the air.

Sorry, but that isn't how it is. We are citizens of heaven and our love for our Creator/Saviour and our new life with Him began the moment we asked His forgiveness. If we don't love Him here, we won't get the opportunity to love Him there. According to Matthew 22:35–38, loving God is absolutely the most important thing we can do on this earth, so it is probably a good idea to learn as much about it as we can, right? Wrong!

Do you really think it's possible to learn about love? Love is defined in Webster's as

> a powerful emotion felt for another person manifesting itself in deep affection, devotion, or sexual desire//the object of this emotion//God's regard for His creatures// charity (the virtue).

The definition really doesn't lend itself to something we can achieve through study or bookwork. Although I have heard and read a lot about her, I never met Mother Teresa of India. I admired her achievements, perseverance, courage and evident faith, but I never loved her because I never knew her.

Many people are the same way with Jesus, including some biblical scholars and evangelical ministers. They spend years studying Scripture, and hours each week reading commentaries and essays and books about Christ and His life, but they never take the time to get to know the real Christ. They don't know Him, even though they know all about Him, because they never spend time with Him or talk with Him. It isn't as though He's inaccessible.

> *And Jesus came and spoke to them, saying, "All authority has been given to Me in heaven and on earth. Go therefore and make disciples of all the nations, baptizing them in the name of the Father and of the Son and of the Holy Spirit, teaching them to observe all things that I have commanded you; and lo, I am with you always, even to the end of the age." Amen.*
>
> —Matthew 28:18–20

Matthew 22 teaches us that there are three separate aspects of love: heart, soul, and mind.

"I love you" are the words we use to try and convey the depths of emotion we feel for another individual. This is the love Webster was trying to define earlier. As any love-stricken individual can attest, it's a feeling that cannot be expressed adequately in words. Thus the truest expression for heart love becomes our actions. Whether it be flowers, diamonds, a cloak spread across a puddle to prevent a woman from getting her feet wet (as Walter Raleigh is alleged to have done for Elizabeth I of England), or a sleepless vigil beside the bed of a sick child, heart love is best expressed through acts rather than words.

The following limerick is as true in our relationship with God as it is in our relationships with others. It takes a very mature love to stand the stress of prolonged separation without dulling or growing cold.

Absence makes the heart grow fonder,
No, absence causes the eyes to wander.

It isn't possible for our love for someone to flourish unless we spend time with him and put a great deal of effort into the relationship. Loving God is no different. Reading daily devotionals and spending five minutes on one's knees plus church on Sunday mornings isn't going to awaken the emotional instincts that the definition of love implies. Does the following quote sound like your relationship with Christ?

O my dove, in the clefts of the rock, in the secret places of the cliff, let
me see your face, let me hear your voice; for your voice is sweet, and
your face is lovely.

—Song of Songs 2:14

Not the normal phraseology you hear from the pulpit on Sunday morning, is it? Then again, look back at our definition of love: "a powerful emotion felt for another person manifesting itself in deep affection, devotion."

Consider the words to the hymn "How Great Thou Art."

Oh Lord my God! When I in awesome wonder
Consider all the worlds Thy hands have made,
I see the stars, I hear the rolling thunder,
Thy power throughout the universe displayed.

Then sings my soul, my Saviour God, to Thee
How great Thou art, how great Thou art![4]

The emotion and conviction of the author is evident in every phrase. These strong words do not reflect our standard approach to God.

It is possible that our greatest difficulty in obeying this first commandment is our own "practical" outlook on life. If we can't see it, hear it, touch it or taste it, we have a great deal of difficulty accepting it as real. We seem to believe that the Kingdom of Heaven is for when we die and that it isn't really possible to love God until we actually see Him after we die. Well, Jesus put the lie to that argument in one of His parables:

Again, the kingdom of heaven is like treasure hidden in a field, which a man found and hid; and for joy over it he goes and sells all that he has and buys that field. Again, the kingdom of heaven is like a merchant seeking beautiful pearls, who, when he had found one pearl of great price, went and sold all that he had and bought it.

—Matthew 13:44–46

To summarize, the Kingdom of Heaven is to be sought now. It is a treasure worth far more than the assets we have on hand. It's worth our every effort to gain the Kingdom.

The Apostle Paul put it all in one verse: *"Pursue love, and desire spiritual gifts"* (1 Corinthians 14:1). This is the verse that immediately follows the so-called love chapter. Everything else is okay, but the most important thing to pursue is love. It is worth the effort.

How emotional do you get when you think about Christ? Does your love for God meet the admittedly inadequate definition from Webster's? Do you even know Him well enough to be able to truly say that you love Him?

Something to think about!

---

4 "How Great Thou Art," Carl Gustav Boberg (1885).

Chapter 15

The Need to Know

QUESTION: WHAT DID ALEXANDER GRAHAM BELL INVENT?

That's a no-brainer, right? He invented the telephone. What a dumb question. The telephone was patented around 1876, when he was thirty. He came up with his first bright idea when he was only twelve: a device that thrashed and separated grain. It evidently worked well. Apart from the telephone, he developed the hydrofoil and his boat, the Bras D'Or, set a speed record that lasted for ten years. He invented the telephone, a metal jacket to assist in breathing, the selenium battery, the audiometer to detect minor hearing problems, a device to locate icebergs, investigations on how to separate salt from seawater, and worked on finding alternative fuels. He patented a working phonograph and a prototype photo phone—or radiotelephone, as it is called now. He contributed to the development of the first aeroplane that utilized a rudder and ailerons; the Wright brothers used wing warping to provide directional control. Bell died in 1922, leaving a legacy of thirty different patents.

He was a firm believer in self-education. Here's what he had to say:

> *The education of the mind is after all, not a question of remembering facts which someone else gives us. The mind should conduct its own education to a larger extent. And it cannot do this unless it thinks for itself. A mind that does not reason is comparatively useless.*

I have given the subject of self-education a great deal of thought and have evolved what you might call a "Rule of Three" in regard to it. The rule is simply this: "Observe! Remember! Compare!"[5]

Most fact-based classroom lessons that I can recall required nothing more than a regurgitation of facts as recited by the teacher or dredged up out of a textbook, with one exception: my Grade Eight history lessons centred on Canada from discovery to confederation in 1867. One of the most significant events was the Battle for Quebec, between the English and their allies and the French and theirs. Instead of simply reiterating the available events, the teacher brought in materials and had us construct a large one-by-two-meter diorama identifying the fortifications, the strengths and weaknesses of both positions, and the strategies needed to ensure victory for (a) the British, or b) the French. It took a lot of research by all members of the class and taught us more about learning than any lecture could have done. By the time the class finished, we were confident in our knowledge and able to rationally explain our positions to anyone. It's relatively simple to memorize facts: understanding comes with questioning, and then doing it ourselves.

Of the three steps outlined by Mr. Bell, the most difficult is observation, yet this is the only way to accumulate material for knowledge. First of all, it involves work. You must read, study, look about, and finally ask questions. Few people have the necessary humility to ask questions. It is more satisfying to one's vanity to proffer information instead. Yet the most remarkable (and interesting) people in the world are eternal collectors of information.

Ignorance is not bliss! When it comes to Scripture, God, eternity, and yes, Satan as well, it is crucially important to know, and knowing is more than being able to reproduce facts upon demand.

Here's a simple example. A well-intentioned missionary gathered together the children in the village where she was working and taught them John 3:16 until each child could recite it perfectly (complete with accent). Unfortunately for the spiritual well-being of the children, she

---

5 *Reader's Digest Classic Reads 2012* (Montreal, QC: Reader's Digest Canada, 2012), 124.

taught them to recite it in English. Since no one in the village actually understood English, all of that study was for naught.

Real learning can be defined as acquiring awareness of one's lack of knowledge. Take a moment to read Deuteronomy 6. In this chapter, Moses is preparing the Israelites for their invasion of Canaan. He knows that they will encounter idolatry, polygamy, prostitution, and a host of other temptations they have been insulated from during their years of wandering. To preserve their beliefs and way of life, Moses tells the parents to instruct their children carefully so that they might know. How often in the gospels does Jesus rebuke the church leaders? He asks, "Don't you know? Haven't you read in the law...?"

Paul, Peter, John, and probably others of the early church leaders maintained a correspondence with the new churches scattered throughout the Roman Empire. Paul's statements to the Colossians spell out the reason:

> *For this reason we also, since the day we heard it, do not cease to pray for you, and to ask that you may be filled with the knowledge of His will in all wisdom and spiritual understanding; that you may walk worthy of the Lord, fully pleasing Him, being fruitful in every good work and increasing in the knowledge of God.*
>
> —Colossians 1:9–10

Why should we study? Here is the reason John gave.

> *Beloved, do not believe every spirit, but test the spirits to see whether they are from God, because many false prophets have gone out into the world.*
>
> —1 John 4:1, NASB

Here are six benefits of being spiritually knowledgeable:

1. Knowledge gives substance to faith.
2. Knowledge gives us something to fall back on when we're confronted by problems.
3. Knowledge gives us confidence in using Scripture.

4. Knowledge equips us to identify error.
5. Knowledge contributes to our confidence.
6. Knowledge helps stamp out fear and superstition.

It's an impressive list, is it not? But there is still one very important aspect that is missing. The prophet Hosea lived just prior to the fall of Israel. In his book, he foretold the hardships Israel would shortly undergo, and he gives the reason why. Pay particular attention to Hosea 1:6, below. It specifically identifies the church leaders as being responsible.

If one were to remove any identification with Israel, Hosea could be describing Canada or Belgium, Uganda or the U.S., or maybe your country. As I read it, our lack of spiritual knowledge and discernment is at least partially responsible for the mess our nations are in.

> *Listen to the word of the Lord, O sons of Israel, for the Lord has a case against the inhabitants of the land, because there is no faithfulness or kindness or knowledge of God in the land. There is swearing, deception, murder, stealing and adultery. They employ violence, so that bloodshed follows bloodshed. Therefore the land mourns, and everyone who lives in it languishes along with the beasts of the field and the birds of the sky, and also the fish of the sea disappear. Yet let no one find fault, and let none offer reproof; for your people are like those who contend with the priest. So you will stumble by day, and the prophet also will stumble with you by night; and I will destroy your mother.* My people are destroyed for lack of knowledge. Because you have rejected knowledge, I also will reject you from being My priest. Since you have forgotten the law of your God, I also will forget your children.
>
> —Hosea 4:1–6, NASB (emphasis added)

That is something to think about!

Chapter 16

Sense and Nonsense about the Will of God

Do you like this chapter's title? Catchy, isn't it? Unfortunately, when it comes to our understanding of the will of God, it accurately reflects how we think. Many of us just don't know the first thing regarding the means of determining God's will for our lives. That's a problem, because if we truly desire to live a life that honours God, we must prayerfully seek His input and approval as we make the plans and decisions that shape our lives. Proverbs contains God's wisdom regarding many of the issues of life, including personal ethics, marriage, parenting, and money management.

Proverbs 3:5–6 is one of the most familiar passages in the Bible:

> *Trust in the Lord with all your heart and do not lean on your own understanding. In all your ways acknowledge Him, and He will make your paths straight.*
> —Proverbs 3:5–6, NASB

This passage of Scripture speaks to our hearts because it addresses a need we all feel—the need for divine guidance. Unfortunately, when it comes to God's will, we are often confronted with a lot of misinformation and confusing teaching. As a result, many Christians make wrong turns and end up in dead-end streets because they don't understand how God guides His children.

Sometimes a verse can become so familiar to us that we fail to stop and think about what it's really saying. Before taking a closer look at these verses, it's important to dispel some of the misconceptions people have about the will of God.

Here are three common myths people believe.

Misconception 1:
God wants me to know the future.

There is something about human nature that causes us to be curious about what's around the corner. We would like to know what the future holds so that we can plan for it. But God doesn't guide us by revealing what our life will be like a month from now or a year from now.

Psalm 119:105 paints a clear picture of how God guides us. It tells us that God's Word is *"a lamp to my feet and a light to my path."*

This verse gives us a picture of someone walking along a dark path with enough light to guide him one step at a time. That's how God guides us: He provides us with the wisdom and direction we need for the next step.

Does God know what will happen tomorrow? Of course He does. He knows what the future holds for each one of us, but these things are hidden from us. Deuteronomy 29:29 says that *"the secret things belong to the Lord our God..."* Dwelling upon the future just distracts us from solving the problems of today. Matthew 6:34 say, *"So do not worry about tomorrow; for tomorrow will care for itself. Each day has enough trouble of its own"* (NASB).

Our responsibility is to trust Him one step at a time, to trust Him moment-by-moment and day-by-day. When we do that, God provides us with the guidance we need for our present circumstances.

Misconception 2:
God's highest goal is my personal happiness.

Today, many Christians buy into this false idea. They believe that God's supreme goal is to make them happy. It sounds good, doesn't it? "God wants me to happy." "God wants me to be fulfilled." This kind of thinking has been used to justify all kinds of sinful and self-centred behaviour.

One of the discussion topics on *Christianity Today*'s website last year dealt with the issues of divorce and remarriage within the church. At issue was the fact that even within Christian circles, it's not uncommon for people to divorce their spouse so they can marry someone else in the church. The explanation given: "because God wants us to be happy."

Yes, God wants to fill us with joy, peace, and other blessings, but personal happiness can never be the primary guiding force in our life. We need to be guided by the Holy Spirit and a sincere desire to do what is right and pleasing in God's eyes. God's plan for our lives never includes breaking one of His commandments, and doing so will never lead to greater joy and contentment.

Being in the will of God is not necessarily the easiest road to take. It might mean getting out of our comfort zone. It might mean facing a challenging situation that God uses to shape our faith. God's supreme goal for us is holiness and maturity in our faith. 1 Thessalonians 4 states plainly that God's will is for us to be holy.

Romans 8:29 states that God's purpose is to conform us into the likeness of Christ. God takes the good and bad circumstances of our lives and uses them to shape our faith so that we become a greater reflection of His Son. That is God's will for every believer.

Misconception 3: God's will is hard to find.

At times, we struggle with making difficult decisions because God doesn't make everything crystal clear. We think that God's will is hard to find, but this is not the biblical perspective. God will provide us with guidance as long as we sincerely desire to do His will. Psalm 32:8 contains the following divine promise: *"I will instruct you and teach you in the way you should go; I will counsel you with My eye upon you"* (NASB).

Unfortunately, we sometimes run into problems because we want God to sanction our own plans and to bless our own desires, rather than seeking to follow through on what He wants us to do.

According to Webster's Dictionary, tradition is the

handing down of beliefs, customs and practices from one generation to another. A tradition is a long-established or inherited way of thinking and acting.

Although traditions have their place, the Bible instructs us to be led by God, as opposed to being led by traditions or cultural values.

How does the Lord guide us? Proverbs 3:5–6 provides a short course on receiving divine guidance. Let's look at three key principles we find in these two verses:

Principle 1:
Receive God's guidance and put your full confidence in the Lord.

The first part of verse 5 tells us to trust in the Lord. When we think of putting our trust in something, we think of relying on someone or putting our confidence in something. But the Hebrew word for trust is much stronger. The Hebrew word for trust literally means to rest our full weight upon something. It conveys the idea of depending completely on the Lord without reservation. God guides the person who depends upon Him and walks by faith.

Principle 2:
Don't lean on your own ability to figure things out.

The second part of verse 5 tells us to lean not on our own understanding. We lean on something when we are not strong enough to stand alone. The implication is that we need divine guidance because human wisdom is limited. Listen to Proverbs 28:26: *"He who trusts in himself is a fool, but he who walks in wisdom is kept safe"* (NIV).

God has not left us to our own devices. He has promised to give us direction and wisdom when we ask for it. His Word gives us practical instruction for living wisely and successfully. He has given us His Spirit to equip us and lead us. Following the will of God means that we must take the commands and principles found in God's Word and apply them to our day-to-day lives.

Principle 3:
Know God deeply and intimately.

Proverbs 3:6 says, *"In all your ways acknowledge Him, and He will make your paths straight."* In the Hebrew, the word translated "acknowledge" means to know someone or something deeply and intimately. In essence, this verse is saying that having a personal knowledge of God is a prerequisite to receiving divine guidance. We must know Him through personal experience before God can guide us.

An interesting transformation occurs in a husband and wife as their marriage matures with time: they begin to know each other at such a deep level that sometimes they know what the other person is thinking, or they know what the other person is about to say before they say it. This is due to the intimate knowledge they acquire of one another, a knowledge that can only come with time and effort.

For the same reasons, our understanding of God's desires in our lives becomes more transparent. Proverbs 3:6 is literally saying that we should strive to know God as deeply as we can. We must discipline ourselves to pray consistently, read His Word and be challenged by biblical teaching, and step out in faith and obedience. In these ways, we deepen our relationship with God. As Jesus said in Matthew 6:33, *"But seek first the kingdom of God..."*

Our society defines success in terms of having lots of money in the bank, a big house, a professional degree, and so on. God defines success in terms of our faithfulness to Him. Proverbs 3 provides three promises to those who are faithful to God.

Promise 1:
God will guide you as you surrender your life to Him.

Proverbs 3:6 tells us that when we acknowledge God in all our ways, He will make our paths straight. If we submit ourselves to the rule of God in our lives, He will provide us with the direction and wisdom we need.

Promise 2:
God's guidance arises out of your relationship with Christ.

Receiving divine guidance begins with having an ongoing relationship with Jesus. We often look at God's will as a destination. However, we should look at God's will as something we walk in day by day. To walk in the will of God is to follow Christ faithfully and obediently on a daily basis.

Promise 3:
God will reveal what you need to know, when you need to know it.

In Acts 20:23, the Apostle Paul said, *"I only know that in every city the Holy Spirit warns me that prison and hardships are facing me"* (NIV).

The Spirit of God had prepared Paul to expect hardship, but God hadn't revealed the exact details. Like Paul, we must trust that God will lead us with enough information to help us face our circumstances, whatever they may be.

If our desire is to walk in the will of God, we must heed the message of Proverbs 3:5–6 (my paraphrase):

In all your ways, strive to know God deeply and submit your will to Him. And He will direct your paths.

Something to think about!

Chapter 17

Black-and-White or Colour?

DO YOU RECALL ALL THAT STUFF A COUPLE OF CHAPTERS BACK ABOUT knowledge and learning? It's important to learn, but knowledge by itself is dangerous. Look at what Paul had to say about it:

> *If I have the gift of prophecy, and know all mysteries and all knowledge; and if I have all faith, so as to remove mountains, but do not have love, I am nothing.*
>
> —1 Corinthians 13:2, NASB

To my mind, there is no worse person to talk to than a person who has made a career out of accumulating knowledge. You know the one. Mention football and he'll rhyme off the statistics for the strikers on every team playing in the European Cup. He knows every law of gravity ever written and can look at the sky and tell you the names and altitudes of every different cloud layer visible.

How about theology? He has an argument and an answer for everything. He knows the names and correct pronunciation of every book of the Bible and can recite whole chapters when asked (and even when not asked). Everything to him is black and white. I suspect if you opened his mind, you would find everything filed under heading, sub-heading, then bullet 1, 2, 3, n where n is the total number of facts available for each topic. If the statement you utter doesn't fit into one of those bullets, it's flat-out wrong.

Does that sound like someone you know? They are good people with firm beliefs and total commitment to the truth, but they have no joy and no colour in their lives. The problem with knowledge is that it contains nothing but information. There is no life in it. If we study doctrine for the sake of learning more, more knowledge is all we will gain. We will know a whole bunch more but we won't get to know the person behind the knowledge. The study of doctrine should enhance our walk with God. It should also improve our relationships with people around us.

In Paul's description of love (1 Corinthians 13:2), the knowledge referred to is the type we have just been talking about. It is factual, doctrinal, theological, and biblical—and it must be paired with love. Without love, the facts are empty.

Life is not two-dimensional, and neither is God. He is full of beauty, colour, variety, and depth, and He is overflowing with love and grace. So learning about God should result in greater appreciation and understanding of these aspects and a greater desire to develop them in our own character. If it doesn't, then we need to change the focus of our studies. We need to go beyond knowledge and work upon our discernment.

To discern means to perceive with the mind. It goes beyond visual observation to the things happening behind the scenes. It concerns the causes and effects rather than the action itself. It sees the pain and suffering hidden behind the joke, or the easy camaraderie. It understands! On the negative side, it triggers an alert when something appears to be missing or not quite in order. In 1 John 4:1, we are told to check things out to see if they are from God. We are told to look in the corners to see if something is not quite right with the testimony we are hearing or the "truth" that is being taught:

> *Beloved, do not believe every spirit, but test the spirits to see whether they are from God, because many false prophets have gone out into the world.* (NASB)

Just because the evangelist is on TV, or just because he's entitled to the title "Doctor," doesn't mean he is right. No person, no matter how sincere, is in possession of all the truth. In Acts, we encounter the church in Berea which scrutinized the words of Paul to determine whether they were aligned with the Scripture. For this, they were commended. Now, if God was pleased that people were testing Paul, then the words I write should certainly be put under close scrutiny as well, as should those we hear from the pulpit every week. Questioning a speaker doesn't imply that you are in doubt as to their veracity. Look at the attitude of the Bereans in Acts 17:11–12:

> *Now these were more noble-minded than those in Thessalonica, for they received the word with great eagerness, examining the Scriptures daily to see whether these things were so. Therefore many of them believed, along with a number of prominent Greek women and men.* (NASB)

These folks were super enthusiastic. They wanted more. But why did they believe the words of Paul and Silas? They were in harmony with those in Scripture. That's discernment, and it's positive.

In 3 John, the Apostle introduces us to a believer named Diotrephes. He was a power hungry, domineering bully. Notice, though, that John doesn't question either his faith or his knowledge. If Diotrephes had been lacking in these areas, it is probable that John would have mentioned it. It was Diotrephes' desire to run things his way that got him in hot water and caused John to censure him. Diotrephes lacked discernment. He was tactless, lacked grace, and certainly was a little weak in the 'love thy neighbour' department.

The church in Corinth is a fine example of an entire congregation that lacked discernment. In 1 Corinthians 1,

> *I thank my God always concerning you for the grace of God which was given you in Christ Jesus, that in everything you were enriched in Him, in all speech and all knowledge, even as the testimony concerning Christ was confirmed in you, so that you are not lacking in any gift, awaiting eagerly the revelation of our Lord Jesus Christ, who will also confirm you to the end, blameless in the day of our Lord Jesus Christ.*
> —1 Corinthians 1:4–8, NASB

At first glance, this is a great church. It is doctrinally sound and the people are intelligent and knowledgeable, eagerly awaiting

Christ's return and not lacking in any spiritual gift. The church was founded by Paul and had one of the greatest early ministers (Apollo) as its primary teacher when Paul left. So what was their problem? They couldn't get along:

> *Now I exhort you, brethren, by the name of our Lord Jesus Christ, that you all agree and that there be no divisions among you, but that you be made complete in the same mind and in the same judgment. For I have been informed concerning you, my brethren, by Chloe's people, that there are quarrels among you.*
> —1 Corinthians 1:10–11, NASB

It sounds like they were constantly at each other's throats. They were quarrelling like a pack of children over who goes first. They had knowledge, but they weren't keeping it in perspective. They had divided into cliques—those who were saved under Paul's ministry and those who had been baptized by Apollos were lording it over those who had not. Paul enlarges upon the issue:

> *...for you are still fleshly. For since there is jealousy and strife among you, are you not fleshly, and are you not walking like mere men? For when one says, "I am of Paul," and another, "I am of Apollos," are you not mere men? What then is Apollos? And what is Paul? Servants through whom you believed, even as the Lord gave opportunity to each one. I planted, Apollos watered, but God was causing the growth. So then neither the one who plants nor the one who waters is anything, but God who causes the growth.*
> —1 Corinthians 3:3–7, NASB

This bunch of juveniles were lacking in discernment. They had failed to balance their knowledge with grace and love. Consequently, their lives had not been changed by the knowledge they had absorbed. As a side note, observe what Paul had to say about his and Apollos' efforts. It isn't us but God who accomplishes things. In other words, don't worship the preacher—he's only the messenger and he can be wrong. Look at God instead.

In 1 Corinthians 8, we encounter yet another truth regarding knowledge:

> *Knowledge makes arrogant, but love edifies. If anyone supposes that he knows anything, he has not yet known as he ought to know.*
>
> —1 Corinthians 8:1–2, NASB

As you can see, discernment is truly the understanding that lies beneath knowledge.

Two principles will keep it all in perspective. First, knowledge should make God more alive and real. Second, no one man has a cornerstone on truth, but God does. Test the word against Scripture. No specific interpretation is correct. If the Bereans thought that the words of Paul and Silas should be compared to Scripture, how much more should those we hear today be subjected to the same scrutiny?

Gaining knowledge and growing in wisdom is important. We need to know why we believe what we believe. But love and grace is equally important. The Bible says,

> *But as you abound in everything—in faith, in speech, in knowledge, in all diligence, and in your love for us—see that you abound in this grace also.*
>
> —2 Corinthians 8:7

> *...but grow in the grace and knowledge of our Lord and Savior Jesus Christ. To Him be the glory both now and forever. Amen.*
>
> —2 Peter 3:18

Something to think about!

Chapter 18

Secrets to Contentment

Dear Pastor,

Sure have been enjoying your sermons lately. The wife and I keep coming back and keep finding out new things about our faith. Keep up the good work. Haven't had much to complain about, either. Work is going good, the plant just put on a second shift and I got that promotion to shift boss so everything there is going good. Even the kids are cooperating these days. That youth pastor you talked the board into hiring has done wonders for their interest in church. Still can't get 'em up for Sunday School, but there's no trouble whatsoever with their being ready for Youth Time on Fridays. What a change!

So why am I writing if everything is going so good? Well, it's directly connected with all the good things that are happening. Am I being set up for a big fall? Is God testing me or something with all these good things? There are loads of people in the church who are struggling with plant closures and layoffs, and they have to make do on a whole lot less than we do. Sometimes I feel guilty because I have and they do not. I'm starting to worry, Pastor. Can you help me out?

Sincerely yours,
Third Pew Back, Left-Hand Side

Dear Third Pew.

Your question brings up some interesting thoughts that maybe aren't exactly what you are seeking, but I will start off with them. We will see where it goes from there.

Lots of choruses, hymns, and sermons have been penned on this very topic: "Every Promise in the Book Is Mine," "He Owns the Cattle on a Thousand Hills," and "Count Your Blessings," just to name a couple. Whole rooms are required to hold the volumes explaining why some have and some haven't. There are even folks who will say you haven't because of unbelief, and they quote John 14:13 (*"And whatever you ask in My name, believing, that I will do"*) and James 4:3 (*"You ask and do not receive, because you ask amiss…"*) to prove it.

But this isn't about debating that concept at all. Instead, let's look at a couple of thoughts that are a little less commonly raised in this discussion but appear to me to be more germane. The first is found in 1 Timothy 6:17:

> *Command those who are rich in this present age not to be haughty, nor to trust in uncertain riches but in the living God, who gives us richly all things to enjoy.* (NKJV)

For those who think that lots of prayer and being highly spiritual will help you achieve riches, take a good look at the first part of the verse and don't equate the two. Basically, the message here is: "You didn't do anything to gain what you have, so don't be so stuck up." A parallel thought would be Jesus' comments regarding the guy praying in the temple, thanking God that he was so perfect and not like the moneychanger/tax collector beside the next pillar, beating his breast in agony of repentance.

Now focus on the second half of the verse: *"God… gives us richly all things to enjoy."* It fits with other scriptures that talk about the Christian life as a joyful and abundant life. It is here we commit a major error in concept development. God gives us to enjoy life not to be rich, but to be content. So how much does He give us? The answer is: enough.

Congratulations on your promotion, by the way. But do you remember a couple of years ago when you were trying to run for union steward and you really, really thought this was God's will? You prayed and you fasted and you recruited others to pray for you and with you, and lo and behold, you didn't get the position. You were passed over, and you were bitter and angry about it too. Bob Stuart got it instead and it was six months before you were able to talk about it without cussin' under your breath. You questioned whether God answered practical prayer and I remember you deciding that while God dealt with the spiritual stuff, we are ultimately responsible for our own gains or losses.

But what about Bob? Bob started having to put in sixty-hour weeks and attend seminars and lectures on labour relations. Within a year, the extra time and time away cost him his wife, his kids, and his happiness. Would you have been any different? I think maybe God did answer your prayer and gave you exactly the position you needed to make the bill payments without the extra time. Like Paul said, He gave you to richly enjoy.

Did you know that six months after every big sale at the appliance store, my marriage counselling schedule gets busier? It seems that marriages suffer a lot when big-screen TVs move in and family nights turn into Saturday Night Football evenings. What I'm saying is that not all things come from God. All *good things* come from God, and it is a wise man who knows the difference. We have a lot of things. Are they good things? From a spiritual perspective, I suspect that most of them are neutral, neither good nor bad. New cars and big-screen TVs are not normally gifts from God. In fact, they are probably more often temptation than blessing.

I have good health, a wonderful family, a dearly loved spouse, and a career that has spanned four decades that I have enjoyed immensely. The list could go on and on. These are good things, and God is responsible for all of them.

God doesn't bring sickness or troubles; He allows it. The Evil One is the sole source for bad things. With God's help, we can minimize the detrimental effects of Satan's efforts, although God may decide to allow us to suffer, and yes, die as a result.

In the parable of the talents, there is one portion that we tend to overlook in this age of equal opportunity. When the king was handing out the tasks, he gave to each man according to his own ability. God knows all of our circumstances. He knows what our weaknesses are and He knows all about the great temptation of things: after all, He too was tempted with possessions. So He doesn't give us any more than we can be responsible with.

He isn't the only one handing out the goodies.

I think this is why Paul wrote the following bit to the Philippians, based upon personal experience:

> *Not that I speak in regard to need, for I have learned in whatever state I am, to be content: I know how to be abased, and I know how to abound. Everywhere and in all things I have learned both to be full and to be hungry, both to abound and to suffer need.*
>
> —Philippians 4:11–12

The Lord's Prayer states the principle as well as it can be said: "Lord, make sure that I'm centred where you want me to be and take care of the domestic details to ensure that I stay focussed on Your plan." Or, if you don't recognize my words, try these: *"Thy will be done in earth, as it is in heaven. Give us this day our daily bread"* (Matthew 6:10–11, KJV).

Solomon had it exactly right. He touched on this very subject in Ecclesiastes 5.

> *Here is what I have seen: It is good and fitting for one to eat and drink, and to enjoy the good of all his labor in which he toils under the sun all the days of his life which God gives him; for it is his heritage. As for every man to whom God has given riches and wealth, and given him power to eat of it, to receive his heritage and rejoice in his labor—this is the gift of God. For he will not dwell unduly on the days of his life, because God keeps him busy with the joy of his heart.*
>
> —Ecclesiastes 5:18–20

Eat, drink, work hard, and enjoy your work, for God gave it to you—and if you are achieving wealth and you are in God's will, then rejoice. Those things are His gift to you. If they are His gifts, then you haven't earned them, so use them wisely. The risk in things, as the parable of the rich man so eloquently suggests, is that they tend to separate us from God's will, so that is where you need to focus.

Now, let's look at the reverse side of things. Here's a familiar passage. Focus on the emphasized verses.

> *And the devil said to Him, "If You are the Son of God, command this stone to become bread."*
>
> *But Jesus answered him, saying, "It is written, 'Man shall not live by bread alone, but by every word of God.'"*
>
> *Then the devil, taking Him up on a high mountain, showed Him all the kingdoms of the world in a moment of time. And the devil said to Him, "All this authority I will give You, and their glory; for this has been delivered to me, and I give it to whomever I wish."*
>
> —Luke 4:3–6 (emphasis added)

Power, possessions, and authority are all Satan's to distribute as he sees fit. And he can do it in such a way that we feel we are being truly blessed. After all, he isn't really a red-suited, fork-tailed devil with a pitchfork. In fact, most of us have a hard time telling when he's around most of the time. Normally he's working through people you know and trust, tempting us with good things—often things we have honestly earned like that big-screen TV I mentioned earlier or the promotion that did poor Bob in.

Those so-called good things can lead to separation from our true friends, and create family division and estrangement from God. I think that's what Paul had in mind when he wrote to Timothy:

> *Command those who are rich in this present age not to be haughty, nor to trust in uncertain riches but in the living God...*
>
> —1 Timothy 6:17

If we rely upon that principle, all things will work out for our good.

If I were to choose one word to summarize the entire issue of material blessings, promotions, accumulating wealth, and status, it would be *contentment*. Hope that helps. We will see you on Sunday. Pastor.

Something to think about!

Chapter 19

The God Particle

SCIENCE USED TO SCARE ME A WHOLE LOT! SCIENTISTS WERE THESE REALLY smart people with years of study and experimentation to draw upon, telling me things that I really didn't understand very much. Many of the "facts" they imparted to me seemed to contradict what I had been taught and what I believed to be true from Scripture.

Consequently, I started to compartmentalize—putting issues regarding religion in one area and issues regarding science into another. It wasn't long before I started applying the same process to other issues regarding morality, ethics, and best practices. My thoughts became a tangled conglomeration of fact, fiction, belief, and doubt.

It couldn't continue. It seemed that I had to choose between my faith and what my intellect told me was the truth, and experience had already shown me that this wasn't possible. If the scientists were correct, then aspects of my faith were wrong. More importantly, Scripture itself was in error.

But science is not the enemy of Christ! Pure science is nothing more or less than a search for truth in a logical and systematic manner. In the end, every discovery in the scientific world only serves to emphasise the greatness, complexity, and intricate structural beauty of God's creation.

I was reminded of this the other week when I read about the so-called God particle—not an epithet the scientists involved with the project particularly like, incidentally. According to what I read, earlier on during the search for the particle one of the participating scientists was asked to explain his research to a visiting reporter. On several occasions, the scientist referred to the "Gdmd" particle because of its very elusiveness. A story about a Gdmd particle that no one can find will find little reader appeal, but a story about "the God particle," the foundational building block of the entire universe, will sell papers. And so the name was coined. But I digress!

Here's a very brief explanation of the Higgs boson, or God particle:

The leading explanation is that a field exists that has non-zero strength everywhere—even in otherwise empty space—and that particles acquire mass by interacting with this so-called Higgs field. If this theory is true, a matching particle—the smallest possible excitation of the Higgs field—should also exist and be detectable, providing a crucial test of the theory. Consequently, it has been the target of a long search in particle physics. One of the primary goals of the Large Hadron Collider (LHC) at CERN in Geneva, Switzerland—the most powerful particle accelerator and one of the most complicated scientific instruments ever built—is to test the existence of the Higgs boson and measure its properties which would allow physicists to validate this cornerstone of modern theory.[6]

To put it another way, the Higgs boson (God particle) is the basic building block of all matter. It's too small to see and it doesn't last long enough for us to identify it. Only by guessing where to look, and then measuring the changes in mass for that area, can scientists even tell that a change in matter has occurred at all.

Here's a little history. The Higgs boson is a proposed elementary particle in the standard model of particle physics. Its existence would have profound importance in particle physics, because it would prove the existence of the hypothetical Higgs field—the simplest of several proposed mechanisms for the breaking of the electroweak symmetry, and the means by which elementary particles acquire mass.

The pursuit of knowledge—more particularly, knowledge of how the different parts of this world connect with the other parts of this

---

6 *Higgs Boson "The God Particle,"* Date of access: February 26, 2015 (http://god-particle. webs.com/).

world—has led some very brilliant people to spend a lot of time and money in an attempt to prove or disprove different theories. Hundreds of millions of dollars were spent drilling a tunnel under the Swiss Alps for the express purpose of bouncing a stream of electrons off one another in a controlled, measurable environment in an attempt to confirm or deny the existence of this minute particle. Even though the mathematics indicated that it should be there, it must have taken a lot of faith to carry on for the decades required to conceive the experiments, build the collider, and then search the gigabits of code to locate a tiny anomaly that would indicate that a previously undetected bit of matter had indeed passed by.

Scientists still don't know for sure that the Higgs boson exists. All they know for sure is that something with a non-zero mass has been detected for a tiny fraction of a second. Identifying that minute gravitational fluctuation as an object that exists, however fleetingly, requires faith: at least, that's the language used by the scientists involved. They don't know for sure, but they believe.

Now here's something many Christians don't know! God told us about creation centuries ago. We accept that. But did you realise that He even told us about the Higgs boson? In Hebrews, we read, *"By faith we understand that the worlds were framed by the word of God, so that the things which are seen were not made from things which are visible."* I don't think it's merely coincidence that He caused these words identifying the nuclear basis of all matter to be written in the chapter on faith.

By faith, the universe was spoken into existence, put together out of tiny particles we cannot see today and likely will never be able to see. But we know they are there, for the Bible tells us so, and now science is finally catching up.

Something to think about!

Chapter 20

A Different Look at Philemon

WITHOUT A DOUBT, PHILEMON IS ONE OF MOST UNIQUE BOOKS IN THE NEW Testament. First of all, it's the only personal letter. Whilst Timothy and Titus were addressed to individuals, their contents were intended for distribution, whereas Philemon is directed only to the addressee and his immediate family. Secondly, it's a personal request from Paul that is couched in such a way as to make refusal almost impossible. He deliberately backs Philemon into a corner, although he does so in a most diplomatic manner. Finally, in direct contrast to his other writings, Paul makes no direct theological arguments regarding his normal topics of Kingdom living, justification, faith, or church building.

Paul must have written dozens of letters during his incarceration, so what was the significance of this particular note that caused the early church fathers to include it in the canon of scripture? In my research, I discovered that most commentaries on the text (Adam Clarke's Commentary, Barnes' Notes on the New Testament, Jamieson-Fausset Brown Bible Commentary) focused on the change in Onesimus, his conversion, and the subsequent change in his character and status. All of it is good and relevant, but these same topics are covered elsewhere in Scripture, hardly sufficient reason to incorporate this letter. And then I considered the words of Paul—*"All Scripture is given by inspiration of God..."* (2 Timothy 3:16)—and of Peter—*"for prophecy never came by the will of man, but holy men of God spoke as they were moved by the Holy Spirit"* (2 Peter 1:21)—and I wondered what train of thought I would pursue if the words written by Paul had been uttered by Jesus as one of His lessons to His disciples. In Philemon 4, Paul makes the point that Philemon is constantly on his mind and a part of his prayers. Thus it isn't difficult to imagine him pausing for a moment, his pen in hand, to listen to the words of the Spirit.

When reviewing all the manuscripts available to them, the church fathers would perhaps have recognized the voice of God in Paul's letter and realized that the message transcended the note's stated intent. The following few thoughts are an attempt to examine a part of the rich garden of wisdom that is the letter of Paul to Philemon.

Take a moment to read Philemon. It is copied below in the King James Version, but with a number of deletions. To create the illusion that this epistle was spoken by Jesus, I have deleted specific names where possible. If this had been a lesson from Jesus, it would fit right into Matthew 6 (the Sermon on the Mount). Within the narrative, I generally refer to God as the author, knowing as do you that it was Paul who wrote the letter but believing that the Lord had greater purposes in mind when He advised Paul regarding the wording he used from prison to his beloved friend.

> *2 ...to our beloved Apphia, and Archippus our fellowsoldier, and to the church in thy house: 3 Grace to you, and peace, from God our Father... 4 I thank my [Father], making mention of thee always in my prayers, 5 hearing of thy love and faith, which thou hast toward [Me], and toward all saints; 6 that the communication of thy faith may become effectual by the acknowledging of every good thing which is in you... 7 For we have great joy and consolation in thy love, because the bowels [hearts] of the saints are refreshed by thee, brother. 8 Wherefore, though I might be much bold... to enjoin thee that which is convenient, 9 yet for love's sake I rather beseech thee... 10 for my son Onesimus, whom I have begotten in my bonds: 11 which in time past was to thee unprofitable, but now profitable to thee and to me: 12 whom I have sent again: thou therefore receive him, that is, mine own bowels [heart]: 13 whom I would have retained with me, that in thy stead he might have ministered unto me in the bonds of the gospel: 14 but without thy mind would I do nothing; that thy benefit should not be as it were of necessity, but willingly. 15 For perhaps he therefore departed for a season, that thou shouldest receive him for ever; 16 not*

now as a servant, but above a servant, a brother beloved, specially to me, but how much more unto thee, both in the flesh, and in the Lord? 17 If thou count me therefore a partner, receive him as myself. 18 If he hath wronged thee, or oweth thee ought, put that on mine account... 19 I will repay it: albeit I do not say to thee how thou owest unto me even thine own self besides. 20 Yea, brother, let me have joy of thee: refresh my bowels [heart]... 21 Having confidence in thy obedience I wrote unto thee, knowing that thou wilt also do more than I say. 22 But withal prepare me also a lodging: for I trust that through your prayers I shall be given unto you.

—Philemon 1:2–22, KJV

All done? So instead of having Paul as the author, we assign the narrative to Jesus. But to whom was He speaking or writing? The words of commendation that the author uses make it clear that He is addressing people who are dedicated and consistent followers of Christ. Notably, He finds no fault with their witness. In fact, He goes to great lengths in extolling their exemplary character and testimony. Are we in agreement so far?

It is time to consider the matter of just who is represented by Onesimus. In a broader context, Onesimus could be considered to be both a new believer within a church and one who was previously within the congregation but abandoned it. That he had been or had become of no use to the church is beyond dispute (Philemon 1:11).

Scripture commands us to love one another. The "love your neighbour" commandment is repeated eleven times throughout Scripture, yet in addressing the issue here in Philemon Christ deliberately avoids phrasing His desires in the form of a command. Instead He makes an appeal: "Please do this for me."

What goes beyond love?

Here's a one word answer for you. Acceptance! The church consistently reaches out in love and compassion to people in need, materially and spiritually. A major indicator of a growing church is its success in fulfilling the first commandment, and that certainly wasn't a problem here:

*...hearing of thy love and faith, which thou hast toward the Lord Je-
sus, and toward all saints...*

—Philemon 1:5, KJV

Where the church seems to run into problems is in assimilating people into its inner circle, and that appears to be the issue addressed through this letter.

It is God who saves, and it is God who adds to His church, both globally and specifically. It is true that He employs men as His agents, but His work is not dependent upon them. Instead it is man who's dependent upon God. In verse 11, God specifies the process He wants to put in place.

Churches have difficulty putting new believers and members to work. Certainly we welcome them at the door and take the time to get to know their names or their backgrounds, but then things seem to stop. There are definite exceptions to this rule, of course. If the individual comes highly recommended by her previous church, or is a well-known and respected member of a professional community, or she simply possesses a skill the church desperately needs, we open the doors, but it just isn't possible to welcome her to the missions committee. The last new member on that one was in 1989. Vacancies only occur through death. (Author's note: deliberate exaggeration.) There may also be more personal reasons for our hesitation. Possibly the individual first entered our church as a family hurt by the trauma of divorce, the loss of a job, or a less than pleasant encounter with the law. Perhaps they denigrated our church and what it stood for or ridiculed our youth as they stood outside holding placards protesting abortion. Regardless of the circumstances, it can all be summarized by the heading "I knew you when..."

But things have changed and our Lord is saying, "Here is a person who was of no use to either you or Me. I have changed Him (he was a slave of Satan's) and I am now placing him in your church. There is a job there that he can do. Indeed I have tailored that job specifically for him. Use him there until I call for him to be used elsewhere. When I do, support him and his mission in the same manner that you support me."

By now I'm sure you have reread Philemon a couple of times, trying to align my words with those of our Lord. I am equally certain that you're starting to make the connection. He isn't ordering us to love these people, for we are already committed to doing that; it's part of our nature. He is asking us to do something even harder: to accept this person into our midst as a member of our family.

God is asking us to put aside our knowledge of this individual. Although he may have offended us in the past, stolen from us, left us stranded when we needed him, been arrested for various offenses, or been from a different class or upbringing than ourselves, God wants us to welcome him, not just to our church but into our church family. For the church to be effective, it has to be unified. All parts must function, and they must function together. Unity, theological agreement, love, and acceptance are fundamental to the church. We accept this and work towards it, but then God messes it up by sending a stranger into our midst, someone who doesn't belong or who has harmed us in the past. And God wants us to accept this person, make him part of our close-knit church family and use him in our ministry. He is asking a lot and He knows it. Although God has the authority to order us to do so—after all, this is His world (see Philemon 1:8)—He knows that it isn't possible to force acceptance upon anyone, just as history has proven that you cannot legislate integration. Regardless of the law, we are governed by emotions, by habit, by personal experience, by our neighbour's opinions, and finally by fear. And so He makes it an appeal. He doesn't want us to do it because we have to, but rather because we want to.

He certainly brings out the heavy artillery in His arguments, though. He reminds us of those things He has done for us. Hard to argue with that one, isn't it?

It isn't necessarily intended to give us a guilt trip, but more to place the request in proper perspective. It's a fact of life that as you get older, your memories of the past become brighter and more positive. Bad things are forgotten with time and people fail to realize the degree to which they have personally changed. God is asking that we remember the way we were and welcome this person.

No person can really feel like he belongs if he's constantly looking over his shoulder. Consequently, we have to be sure that we clear our minds regarding our past relations with this new believer. If God can, with the wrongs I have done him, I certainly should be able to follow suit.

> *"...they will all know me, from the least of them to the greatest,"* declares the Lord. *"For I will forgive their wickedness and will remember their sins no more."*
>
> —Jeremiah 31:34, NIV

> *[Love] keeps no record of wrongs.*
>
> —1 Corinthians 13:5, NIV

For this reason, He reminds us of His work on our behalf. At the same time, God makes it clear that it is He who has placed this individual within our Church family.

> *I am sending him back. You therefore receive him, that is, my own heart... receive him as you would me.*
>
> —Philemon 1:12, 17

We come now to what is perhaps the most wonderful part of all. Reread Philemon 1:18. God is saying that although He did not incur the debt or wrongdoings attributed to the individual, He will accept full responsibility for insuring that the debt is not cancelled but is paid in full, as He has already accepted responsibility for the debts of the addressees.

> *"I have blotted out, like a thick cloud, your transgressions, and like a cloud, your sins. Return to Me, for I have redeemed you."* Sing, O heavens, for the Lord has done it!
>
> —Isaiah 44:22–23

To summarize, God reminds us that it is He who builds our church. He reinforces the fact that He has created a position within his church for each person, and there is a task associated with that position. He both commands us and pleads with us to open our hearts and our arms to the believers He places within reach of our influence.

When I first started into this, I took the final few verses (starting from verse 22) as being Paul's personal message to Philemon. As I read and reread this letter, I became more and more appreciative of the wonderful harmony between Paul's simple request to his friend and God's desires for us. He took advantage of every one of Paul's thoughts to re-enforce the message of His Kingdom.

If we accept as fact that Christ is behind every word in Scripture, then verse 22 becomes a warning. As with the parable of the ten bridesmaids, verse 22 reminds us to prepare and be vigilant so as not to be caught unaware—because He *is* coming again. It is a promise, and that truly is something to think about!

Chapter 21

Does Prayer Work?

TIME AND AGAIN AS I CONSIDER WHAT GOD IS LAYING UPON MY HEART TO share with you, one topic keeps coming up: prayer. Prayer is omnipotent. It can do anything God can do.

Ouch! Think that line through, and then read it again! Prayer is omnipotent. It can do anything God can do.

Satan doesn't worry too much about busy Christians. Indeed, I suspect he is often the one encouraging us to get even more involved in church-related "Christian" activities. He has succeeded in convincing the church that our works are of the utmost importance. Churches are well-organised these days. We have big choirs, praise teams, worship leaders, teachers, and treasurers. A great deal of planning goes into each service. The hymns and choruses reflect the theme of the message. We have up-tempo, foot-stomping, hand-clapping gospel music to get us involved, and then quiet, contemplative inspirational tunes to prepare us for the message. We have senior pastors, youth pastors, music directors, pastor-elders, and adult ministry ministers. What we don't often have are prayer meetings. Satan is delighted; in fact, he is ecstatic. He is not afraid of us working. He is *terrified* of us praying.

"But we have monthly prayer vigils," you may say. Good! But what about the other twenty-nine days?

No spiritual movement ever happened as a result of planning or organization. Instead they have all sprung into being as the result of earnest, passionate prayer. The growth of the New Testament church can be accounted for in one word: prayer.

The following verses are all taken from Acts.

Peter, James, John, and Andrew; Philip and Thomas; Bartholomew and Matthew; James the son of Alphaeus and Simon the Zealot; and Judas the son of James. These all continued with one accord in prayer and supplication, with the women and Mary the mother of Jesus, and with His brothers.

—Acts 1:13–14

And they proposed two: Joseph called Barsabas, who was surnamed Justus, and Matthias. And they prayed and said, "You, O Lord, who know the hearts of all, show which of these two You have chosen to take part in this ministry and apostleship from which Judas by transgression fell, that he might go to his own place."

—Acts 1:23–25

And they continued steadfastly in the apostles' doctrine and fellowship, in the breaking of bread, and in prayers.

—Acts 2:42

Continue reading through Acts, and you will find the same sequence over and over. First comes prayer, and then comes results.

Today, things have changed. We are convinced that programme and study will provide results. Prayer meetings, if they exist at all, are sops provided for the more traditionally-minded members. Prayer occupies the tail end of group study and is quickly shortened if the meeting is running a little bit late.

So why are we not the praying people we once were? It isn't that we don't care, and it isn't that we aren't involved. Our involvement has never been the problem. In fact, our churches are inundated with Martha wannabes, all encumbered with serving.

Could it be that we need our belief in prayer revived? What do you think? Consider the following statement: prayer not only does us good, but it brings God into action to work unimaginable wonders on the earth. Everyone will agree that prayer does us good, but are we truly convinced that the second part of that statement is true as well? Or do we accept it as long as there's a condition included—for instance, that prayer brings God into action to work unimaginable wonders on the earth *according to His will*?

The most oft-quoted verse regarding God answering prayer is John 14:14: *"If ye will ask any thing in my name, I will do it"* (KJV). It is a very unambiguous statement. Man asks; God does! But the verse immediately raises questions, not the least of which is this: can prayers change God's plans? Now, I haven't been present at the planning sessions in Heaven, but the Bible tells me that prayer is an essential element of God's purposes here. Prayer is more important to our Lord than fundraising or recruitment drives to fill needed positions within the church, because building the church is His job; we simply provide the manual labour. Matthew 9:38 reads, *"Pray ye therefore the Lord of the harvest, that he will send forth labourers into his harvest"* (KJV). From this verse, it would seem that it is our responsibility to pray for the workers and His responsibility to supply them. At the same time, it is safe to assume that the Lord won't send the labourers until and unless we ask for them.

But what about God changing plans in response to our petitions? Turn to Psalm 106. In these verses, the Hebrew nation is in rebellion against God. God determines to destroy them time and again, but He changes His mind. Why?

> *They forgot God their Savior, Who had done great things in Egypt, wondrous works in the land of Ham, Awesome things by the Red Sea. Therefore He said that He would destroy them, had not Moses His chosen one stood before Him in the breach, to turn away His wrath, lest He destroy them.*
>
> —Psalm 106:21–23

A little later in the same psalm, the Jews are in rebellion once more. Again, God decides to change His plans:

> *Thus they provoked Him to anger with their deeds, and the plague broke out among them. Then Phinehas stood up and intervened, and the plague was stopped.*
>
> —Psalm 106:29–30

Finally, we see the Jewish people crying out in repentance themselves. Again, God changed His plans:

> *Therefore the wrath of the Lord was kindled against His people, so that He abhorred His own inheritance. And He gave them into the hand of the Gentiles, and those who hated them ruled over them. Their enemies also oppressed them, and they were brought into subjection under their hand. Many times He delivered them; but they rebelled in their counsel, and were brought low for their iniquity. Nevertheless He regarded their affliction, when He heard their cry; and for their sake He remembered His covenant, and relented according to the multitude of His mercies.*
>
> —Psalm 106:40–45

Why did He change His mind? People prayed! They interceded before the Lord. There are many more examples throughout the Old Testament.

It would also appear that God really doesn't want to execute judgement, even upon those who appear to deserve it. Abraham argued with God, interceding on behalf of Sodom to the point where God agreed not to destroy the city if only ten righteous people could be found. Now, you can argue that it was a safe bet for God, because He knew even ten was an impossible number for that city. Nevertheless, God was willing to forego judgement. An even more interesting example, however, is found in Ezekiel 22.

> *"So I sought for a man among them who would make a wall, and stand in the gap before Me on behalf of the land, that I should not destroy it; but I found no one. Therefore I have poured out My indignation on them; I have consumed them with the fire of My wrath; and I have recompensed their deeds on their own heads," says the Lord God.*
>
> —Ezekiel 22:30–31

The only conclusion I can draw from these examples is that God is anxious to temper His judgements with mercy—if only we, His people, will intercede on behalf of those who stand condemned. What a solemn thought! What an awesome responsibility. And it doesn't rest upon the shoulders of the pastor or the elders; it is mine, it is yours, and we fulfill this spiritual obligation through prayer.

> *Now it came to pass, as He was praying in a certain place, when He ceased, that one of His disciples said to Him, "Lord, teach us to pray, as John also taught his disciples." So He said to them,* "When you pray, say... "
>
> —Luke 11:1–2 (emphasis added)

The spirit of prayer cannot be borrowed from others. We can't buy the skill, nor is it listed as one of the spiritual fruits. It is not a gift from God, either. Instead, the ability to pray is the result of a one-on-one teaching session with God Himself. Nowhere in Scripture does Christ give teaching lessons or lessons in homiletics. There are no four steps to soul-winning in Scripture. But, as recorded in both Matthew and Luke, Jesus did give us lessons on praying. Evidently, John did as well. Praying is something we learn, and it is a lesson given to each of us. Each of us must individually approach Christ with the same words used in Luke 11: "Lord, teach me to pray."

Prayer does indeed work. The next few chapters will look at other aspects of prayer as illustrated in the sample given to us by Christ Himself. I pray that it will give you something to think about!

Chapter 22

Getting Answers to Prayer

Step 1:
You must be a righteous person.

By faith Elijah obeyed when presented with the evil actions of King Ahab and appeared in the court of the king and commanded that all rainfall stop.

—Hebrews 11:??

DON'T BOTHER LOOKING UP THE REFERENCE. IT ISN'T THERE, ALTHOUGH Hebrews 11 is the faith chapter. Isn't it interesting that one of the premier prophets isn't named in the chapter on faith, although the events of his life might be included in the general endorsement of all the prophets found in the latter half of the chapter? Instead we find Elijah in a chapter on prayer: James 5.

Elijah was a man with a nature like ours, and he prayed earnestly that it would not rain; and it did not rain on the land for three years and six months.

—James 5:17

We have a tendency to think that the men of the Bible were somehow special, but take a look at the first part of the above verse. James 1 identifies the recipients of his letter as the Jewish congregation. In other words, just your normal Christian. James wasn't writing this letter to the remnants of the apostles or to a group of devout Bible scholars, teachers, and saints. Listen to what James had to say about his audience:

> *You have lived on the earth in pleasure and luxury; you have fattened your hearts as in a day of slaughter. You have condemned, you have murdered the just; he does not resist you.*
>
> —James 5:5–6

Elijah was a man just like those Jews, just like you and me. There was nothing special about him. So why were his prayers so effective? The answer is in James 5:16: *"The effective, fervent prayer of a righteous man avails much."* Elijah was a righteous man.

But Romans tells us that there is none who is righteous. Sorry, that isn't quite right. Romans 3 is a quote from Psalms 14, which is talking about a fool. If I may condense the psalm, the reference is to a person who denies God's existence and has become so hardened in his thoughts that no good thought can prevail. If you wish an example, this is precisely what happened with Pharaoh when confronted by Moses. As a matter of fact, a number of verses reference the traits which righteous people show, and God has promised that He will cleanse our unrighteousness from us if we but ask.

Ahab was without a doubt one of the most rotten kings to ever sit on a Hebrew throne. 1 Kings 16:33 says that he did more to provoke the Lord than all the kings who preceded him. The picture of Elijah I see is one of an ordinary man watching his country fall apart. He sees an absolutely evil creature, with his equally rotten spouse, sitting on the throne in Samaria and setting up temples to Astarte and Baal and a host of other foreign gods. It is possible, although not definite, that human sacrifices (particularly of children) were being made. Certainly temple prostitution and drunkenness would have been part of the worship ritual. All of these activities would have caused any righteous man considerable grief. I suspect that, just like Christ did when he looked over Jerusalem the week before His death, Elijah would have wept over what his beloved country was becoming. And so he would have turned to the only refuge he had: Jehovah.

The eyes of the Lord are on the righteous. And His ears are open to their cry.

—Psalms 34:15

So there is Elijah, watching the evil around him and crying out to God. Searching through Scripture, the best description of "righteous" I could come up with is found in the first psalm:

Blessed is the man who walks not in the counsel of the ungodly, nor stands in the path of sinners, nor sits in the seat of the scornful; but his delight is in the law of the Lord, and in His law he meditates day and night. He shall be like a tree planted by the rivers of water, that brings forth its fruit in its season, whose leaf also shall not wither; and whatever he does shall prosper.

—Psalm 1:1–3

Every reference to "righteous" in Scripture is connected with someone who talked to God. Living a righteous life isn't something that just happens overnight. It occurs in people who delight in God's laws and study to follow them all the time.

The description in Psalm 1:3 is beautiful. Israel is a land of mountains, high temperatures, *and deserts*. The thing about mountains is they have no place where water can accumulate; it all runs downhill. Unless the plant is beside a stream, which is the picture here, any water for plants must come from rain. So if it doesn't rain, plants will soon shrivel up and turn brown. If you want your prayers answered, you must establish communication with God now. He's not a 911 operator.

1 Kings 17 doesn't tell us what happened. It just says that Elijah went and stood before Ahab and told him what events were about to occur:

And Elijah the Tishbite, of the inhabitants of Gilead, said to Ahab, "As the Lord God of Israel lives, before whom I stand, there shall not be dew nor rain these years, except at my word."

—1 Kings 17:1

The verses in James give us a clue to the events. Let me spell it out. The rain stopped because Elijah, a righteous man, talked to God and asked Him to stop the rain. Would it have happened otherwise? Logically, the answer to that question is no. James says it stopped because Elijah prayed.

Step 2:
Talk it over with God.

Now, this is the tricky bit. We don't know what he prayed, but we gain a hint as to what those prayers were about. It isn't likely that Elijah, all by himself, said, "Lord, if we stop the rain it might wake Ahab up to his sins." No, that isn't what prayer is about. Prayer is all about conversing with God, discussing problems with Him, and finding His solutions to those problems. So here we have Elijah discussing matters over with God, with whom he is in constant communication.

For the perverse person is an abomination to the Lord, But His secret counsel is with the upright.

—Proverbs 3:32

The first time we have an indication of God talking to Elijah is immediately *after* Elijah talked to Ahab, not before.

Then the word of the Lord came to him, saying, "Get away from here and turn eastward..."

—1 Kings 17:2

Which brings me to rule number three.

Step 3:
If you're in fellowship with God, don't hesitate to act.

Most of Elijah's miracles were performed in the same fashion. Elijah took action knowing that God was with him and that God would support his actions. Want proof? When Elijah raised up the widow's son, he took the dead child from the mother and acted. He depended upon God to respond. It's in verse 22:

> *Then the Lord heard the voice of Elijah; and the soul of the child came back to him, and he revived.*
>
> —1 Kings 17:22

In 2 Kings 1, we have a story of Elijah again commanding fire from Heaven, this time to act in his defence. Twice it happened, and there's no indication that Elijah prayed for it. He just spoke and it happened. Instead we find God speaking to him through His angel only after the third captain of the guards approached Elijah with the acknowledgement that he was indeed a Man of God:

> *And the angel of the Lord said to Elijah, "Go down with him; do not be afraid of him."*
>
> —2 Kings 1:15

Want your prayers answered? Here are the three steps:

1. Be a righteous person.
2. Stay in communication with God.
3. Take action.

Something to think about!

Chapter 23

Prayer

THE JEWISH NATION KNEW ABOUT PRAYER. THE NINTH HOUR IN THE temple (3:00 p.m.) was the hour of prayer. Prayer shawls and phylacteries were symbols of reverence and deference to God. Yet the disciples, who had been brought up in this culture and had been introduced to prayer through lessons in the synagogue from an early age, had observed something different in the communication Jesus had with the Father. Only one other person had been able to make that impression on them, John the Baptist, so they turned to Jesus and asked Him straight out: "Lord, teach us. Show us how we too can converse with the Father in the intimate and wonderful way that you do."

But before anyone can learn to pray, he needs to understand what prayer actually is and isn't. Prayer is the term given to the conversations we enter into with God. Prayer is the entitlement of all believers. Think of it like a giant telephone company. Adam and Eve were created with the ability to communicate with God. He made them that way. We are hardwired with this same faculty, but because of sin, the connections between Heaven and the individual have never been completed. Salvation completes those connections.

This chapter's reference text comes from Matthew 6. The Sermon on the Mount was Jesus' most comprehensive lesson on practical daily living, and His words on prayer are all we really need to know.

And when you pray, you shall not be like the hypocrites. For they love to pray standing in the synagogues and on the corners of the streets, that they may be seen by men. Assuredly, I say to you, they have their reward. But you, when you pray, go into your room, and when you have shut your door, pray to your Father who is in the secret place; and your Father who sees in secret will reward you openly.

And when you pray, do not use vain repetitions as the heathen do. For they think that they will be heard for their many words. Therefore do not be like them. For your Father knows the things you have need of before you ask Him.

In this manner, therefore, pray: Our Father in heaven, Hallowed be Your name. Your kingdom come. Your will be done on earth as it is in heaven. Give us this day our daily bread. And forgive us our debts, as we forgive our debtors. And do not lead us into temptation, but deliver us from the evil one. For Yours is the kingdom and the power and the glory forever. Amen.

For if you forgive men their trespasses, your heavenly Father will also forgive you. But if you do not forgive men their trespasses, neither will your Father forgive your trespasses.

—Matthew 6:5–15

Setting the Scene

It's time to set the scene for prayer. Although any time is a good time to talk with God, the setting for those intimate times with Him is very important. First of all, prayer is private. Listen to what the Matthew passage says: "Go into your room and shut the door." Does this mean we are not to pray in public? Scripture recounts many instances when the church gathered together for prayer. Two memorable instances took place: when Peter walked out of prison, and before Pentecost. But the principles we're discussing today were still followed.

Before Pentecost, Scripture tells us that the disciples, the women, Mary the mother of Jesus, and His brothers *"went up into the upper room where they were staying... [and] continued with one accord in prayer and supplication"* (Acts 1:13–14). Their prayer was private. Only the believers were present. Prayer is our privilege, and it is only accorded to believers. The link between man and God has been reconnected only in us. From all others, Jesus is waiting to hear the words "God, be merciful to me, a sinner." When He hears those words, He immediately completes another permanent installation.

The prayer was unified. When the early church got together for prayer, they stayed with the script—and yes, that means there should be an agenda to enable each person to pray knowledgeably with the one who is verbalizing for the group.

Interestingly, the author distinguishes between conversation and what we now would term "prayer requests" (to be *"with one accord in prayer and supplication"* [Acts 1:14]). This seems to reinforce the notion that asking for our needs to be met is not the primary purpose for prayer; it is not the purpose for which prayer was intended.

When I look at the Lord's Prayer, I find that only a single line is devoted to my personal needs: "Give us this day our daily bread." Except for this single reference, the prayer focuses upon my spiritual well-being and the expansion of God's Kingdom. Prayer is intended as a conversation with God, not as an access code for some form of celestial ATM.

Motivation is important. Jesus recognized the authority and offices of the scribes and Pharisees. In Matthew 23, He commanded His followers to listen to and obey their teachings but not to copy their actions—*"for they say, and do not do"* (Matthew 23:3). They prayed for the sheer joy of listening to their own sonorous tones and to steal from widows while pretending to make intercession for them (Matthew 6:5, 23:14). The pleasure of hearing their voices resonate through the temple was the only reward they would receive. Their modern-day counterparts, incidentally, are the chaps who flood the internet with YouTube videos or are always first to sing on a karaoke night (and shouldn't).

Our prayers should be brief. Jesus says that God knows the things we need before we speak, so once we utter them we have said enough. This does not mean that we shouldn't spend a lot of time in prayer. In fact, the opposite is true. But prayer is conversation, and conversation requires a minimum of two people talking to each other. When I suggest that our prayers should be brief, I mean that we need to spend a whole lot more time listening and a whole lot less time talking. We know that God listens to us, but I'm afraid that very often we forget to listen to Him.

Finally, when we pray, we should be comfortable. There is no reason why we should stand on one foot or sit on a chair of nails when we pray. Being uncomfortable can only cause us to shorten our time of prayer simply to end the discomfort.

With just four words—*"Our Father in heaven"*—Jesus effectively put an end to 2,500 years of Jewish tradition. The name of God was never mentioned even in prayer, yet here was the self-declared Son of God giving His followers permission to address God as "Father," a carefully chosen word. "Father" conjures up thoughts of a family patriarch sitting in the place of honour at the head of the room, surrounded by his children and their spouses, and by his grandchildren as well. It combines love with respect and honour.

It is not synonymous with "Hi, God." Although He is our Father as a result of our rebirth, this is still the ruler of the universe that we are addressing. I would never dream of entering Buckingham Palace and greeting Her Majesty with a hearty "Hi, Liz!" How much greater is God?

Any tour of Europe would be incomplete if it didn't include one of the great houses: Kronsberg, Fredrikshaven, Rosenburg, the Vatican, Versailles, and Schonbrunn, just to name a few. These are truly magnificent testimonials to their architects, but more importantly to the monarchs who inspired their construction.

Isaiah 6:1 describes the throne room in Heaven. It is Versailles multiplied a thousand fold. When Isaiah saw it, he cried out, "I am unclean. My lips are unclean. I am not worthy." Think of some of the songs and choruses that we sing: "How Majestic Is Thy Name in All the Earth," "How Great Thou Art, "I Stand Amazed in the Presence," and on and on. We sing praises to Almighty God and then we have the audacity to address this holy, all-powerful God as if He were the guy next door and we want to borrow his lawnmower.

This diminishment of God through familiarity is one of Satan's favourite weapons that he uses to interfere with one's prayer life. There is an expression in English that says familiarity breeds contempt. Many, many years ago, my high school had a custodian who resembled Phil Silvers, a well-known TV comedian at the time. Kids laughed at him because of his appearance and accent. Although his

English was good, it was more than a little flavoured with an eastern European tinge. What students didn't know was that this gentleman had escaped from one of the eastern dictatorships, and by doing so he had given up the right to be called Herr Professor. He was a PhD in his homeland and spoke at least five languages fluently. Whilst awaiting accreditation in Canada, he had become a janitor to provide himself a living. Not knowing any better, the students treated him with benign contempt, the same attitude that is often prevalent in our approach to the creator. After all, it's only God.

The story is told of a brash young man in the military who boldly informed a certain sergeant that his name was Norman Hanley Mc-Culloch the Sixth, but that it would be okay for the sergeant to address him as Norm. This statement was met with this terse reply: "My name is Sergeant Major Billingsworth, and you will address me as Sergeant Major." Respect. For centuries, the military has known the role that titles play in establishing an appropriate working relationship.

With prayer, familiarity causes us to lessen the importance of prayer in our minds. This increases the likelihood of prayer becoming nothing more than a habit, thus reducing our expectations. If we don't expect God to answer, rest assured that He won't. Respect also puts my requests into the proper perspective. When all is said and done, I can still talk to Him. Think about it! The omnipresent, omnipotent, omniscient creator of the universe *wants* to sit down and talk with me.

Now that's something to think about!

And He walks with me and He talks with me,
And He tells me I am His own.
And the joy we share as we tarry there
None other has ever known.[7]

---

7 "In the Garden," by C. Austin Miles (1968–1946).

Chapter 24

The Lord's Prayer: The Beginning

FROM THE PREVIOUS CHAPTER, WE KNOW THAT PRAYER IS SIMPLY HAVING A two-way conversation with God. God sent His Son as His direct emissary to proclaim a new covenant and invite us to become citizens of His Kingdom. At the same time, He has declared that citizens of Heaven are also members of His immediate family: eligible to be called sons.

What do you picture when you think of Heaven? If you are like most people, the word Heaven conjures up visions of a location eons away, accessible only after death. It is inhabited by angels (with white feathery wings) and the wispy spirits of ancestors long forgotten. The streets and houses are made of gold and marble respectively, and a magnificent jade wall surrounds the city. Does my image match yours?

In reality, Heaven surrounds us—but in a dimension we cannot see without the direct assistance of God Himself. It's right here, as close to us as the word "here" can possibly convey. It's as close to you as your neighbour's house. Think not? Consider Jacob's dream of a ladder, or staircase, extending into Heaven. Anything longer than a few dozen meters and its upper end would no longer be distinguishable, yet Scripture clearly states that the top reached Heaven and angels were climbing and descending. When Abraham was about to sacrifice Isaac, he was stopped by the voice of the Angel of the Lord calling to him from Heaven. When John baptised Jesus, God voiced His approval from heaven: *"This is My beloved Son, in whom I am well pleased"* (Matthew 3:17).

Heaven is indeed all around us, and that's a comforting thought. Your prayers are not echoing off the walls of the cosmos to a God who's far removed from His creation; instead they are being spoken to the God who is so close that He can hear the faintest whisper.

Now, back to the Lord's Prayer.

Properly understood, the opening words spoken by Jesus were intended to convey this direct and immediate access. When we pray, we should be picturing ourselves sitting in the presence of God, just as we might sit in the living room during a family gathering. Our prayer is in response to the Father asking, "How was your day?" This is the most amazing thing: God *wants* to talk to us.

Hallowed be Thy Name

Certain rules must be followed when addressing any leader. At the very least, a leader is addressed by his rank or position, never by name. No one would ever call the president of the United States "Mr. Obama." It is always "Mr. President." The queen is "Your Majesty." In Daniel 2, we learn the correct way to address the king of Babylon:

> *Then the Chaldeans spoke to the king in Aramaic, "O king, live forever! Tell your servants the dream, and we will give the interpretation."*
> —Daniel 2:4

By addressing a leader in this fashion, we identify them as someone special. It's not intended as flattery but as a means of setting them apart.

But I don't believe this is the thought behind the first line of the Lord's Prayer. "Hallowed" is an old English word for which there are no familiar synonyms to provide a clear explanation. Words like *sacred* or *holy* are part of it, but the notion goes far deeper. If you add the concept of veneration together with holiness, then phrase the whole mix into the first person so that the individual making the statement emphasises the personal aspect of the action, you might begin to fathom the thought behind this verb: "Lord, I honour you and I worship you. I consider as sacred everything about You, and I tremble in fear and stand in awe at the very thought that You care for me. I am a man of unclean lips, and I am not worthy to speak to you." As you can see, it's a struggle to come up with a meaningful comparison—and that's the very reason this phrase is used.

I used to wonder how people could say that they spent hours in prayer. I mean, what are they praying for? Even the largest of churches have a finite number of sick people. I only have a couple of dozen close relatives and friends, and most of them don't confide in me regarding all their problems. Most people are only acquainted with the missions that their own churches sponsor, plus maybe one or two independent interests, so what on earth can they pray about for so long?

Now that is what I used to think, before I really took a look at the Lord's Prayer. It is this phrase that can stretch a two-minute prayer into an hour or more. You don't believe me, do you? Well, read on and we'll see if I can change your mind.

This first phrase enables us to remind ourselves who and what God is. We need this simply because our daily dose of living can be depressing. It can create feelings of doubt and anxiety and cause us to question the very purpose of our existence. In other words, just getting through the day can sometimes be the pits.

So imagine that you're at the end of a really bad shift at work. You sit down for prayer and start reviewing everything that went wrong. Bad idea! Instead, try this: "Hallowed be the Shepherd who has guided me through to this point in time. Hallowed be the One who has provided me with food, shelter, and water. Hallowed be the Counsellor who is waiting to advise me, and who provides me with ideas, patience, and the correct words. Hallowed be the Physician, my Protector..." Get the idea? As you work your way through the names and attributes of God, you can discover that for every problem you've encountered that day, God has the resources to help you overcome it. Shepherd, Counsellor, Physician, Protector... it is all found in the name.

I love music, almost all types of music. I have to say "almost" because I have yet to develop any enthusiasm for opera, rap, or funk. I have shelves full of gospel, old hymns, country and western, folk, symphony, spirituals, and good ol' rock and roll in just about every format you can imagine from seventy-eight records right up through CDs and everything in between. Consequently, I find that music really helps me as I pray this phrase. Think of some of the titles: "A Mighty Fortress Is

Our God," "Majesty, Worship His Majesty," "Lead Me to the Rock," etc. Almost all provide me with some insight into the wonders of God's name—and that's what this portion of prayer is all about. It's about praise, worship, and adoration. There's absolutely nothing wrong with breaking out into song as you sit alone in your room with the world shut out, even if you can't carry a tune. Scripture covers that, you know. "Make a joyful noise..."

But this is only the first line of our prayer. Choruses are great, but a musical programme that features nothing but choruses and ditties is as tedious as a musical programme that features nothing but old hymns and chants. God enjoys music. After all, He gave us that capability. But the intent of praise in prayer is not to flatter Him. God does not have an over-inflated ego, and He certainly doesn't require inadequate expressions of praise and love to help Him get through each day. It's not Him who requires this portion of praise; rather, it's us. Praising God gets our minds off the world and its problems and allows us to focus on things that are positive, things that are uplifting, things that provide us with solutions and answers. In other words, it focuses our attention upon our citizenship in Heaven, its benefits, and its blessings.

So once our minds are firmly focused upon Him, it is time to leave praise and move into the heart of prayer. But not this week! Instead, take some time and think about the names of God. Think about what each of those names means, and their implications regarding both His character and its effect on our own lives. And think about all those songs and choruses you know that illustrate so beautifully the wonders of God. In other words, it's something to think about!

Chapter 25

Thy Kingdom Come

WHEN I STOP, STEP BACK, AND TAKE A REALLY CRITICAL LOOK AT MY NORMAL prayer, I find that it sounds like this: "Father in Heaven, hallowed be Thy name, give us this day our daily bread and forgive my sins, amen." That covers the important points, including a little bit of worship and praise to put God in a better frame of mind to listen—and besides, it makes me feel good. Then, of course, I have to send in my personal wish list. And just to make sure my wishes are heard, I throw in a phrase or two asking for forgiveness.

Sadly, I suspect I'm not the only one who too frequently treats prayer as the input process for an online or telephone mail order catalogue. Requests for forgiveness are included simply because it seems prudent, but I seem to forget the process of asking God to forgive the transgressions of my enemies.

The most serious omission, however, is my failure to include the lines that come right after the introduction: "Thy kingdom come, Thy will be done." These are the lines of commitment. By not including these thoughts, we miss out on the intimacy of prayer, simply because we're keeping ourselves on the periphery of His family.

Bear with me whilst I try to explain.

Consider the words Jesus used. On a superficial level, they seem redundant. There can be little doubt that His kingdom is coming. Revelation, Isaiah, and a number of the other prophets identify the process leading towards the coming millennial reign. Jesus declared that His kingdom was already here. Absolutely nothing happens on earth without His knowledge. So this is not a plea for God to take over.

Rather it is an acknowledgement that God does reign on the earth. At some time in the future—when, we don't know—God will call and His people will respond and leave this world. Satan, his angels, and those who have refused to accept that Christ is the Saviour and believe in Him will be left. Evil will reign, or so it will seem. But there's an already-defined end to that period of time: seven years. Certain events are preordained to occur within those seven years. The plagues mentioned in Revelation will happen. They are from God. The judgements will occur. They are from God. There will be 144,000 witnesses whom Satan will be unable to touch, and there will be those who will turn and cry out to God. And He will hear them. He is, and will remain, supreme.

"Thy will is being done" is how we should approach this portion of the prayer. Not in an abstract manner, but with the petitioning up front and personal: "Heavenly Father, I commit myself to You today. Let my words and actions conform to Your will today." It's in this portion of the prayer that I affirm my commitment to Him, and there is no place in the template where we should insert conditions.

How about this? "Lord God, establish Your kingdom in my life today and let me be ruled by You." It wasn't so long ago that Denmark was an absolute monarchy. The king had the power of life and death over his subjects. Each individual swore fealty to the king and subjugated himself and his family to the king's will. His lands were his, only insofar as the king said "Aye."

That is the meaning behind this phrase. When you start to pray, are you willing to swear fealty to God, even for one day? Without a doubt, Christ in the garden demonstrated the best example of this approach to prayer before his death. "Father, isn't there a better way to solve this problem?" he prayed. "Father, I really don't want to do this," he prayed. "Father, can't you get someone else to do this?" And at the end, "Thy kingdom come, Thy will be done."

One of the hardest things to do as a parent is commit your family in the same manner. "Heavenly Father, Thy will be done in my spouse's life and with my children." There's a lot of potential pain in that prayer. What if God's will and my plans for my family conflict? It's absolutely true that God cares for His own and won't let anything bad happen to them, but that doesn't mean your children won't meet with an accident, suffer a debilitating disease, or be struck done in some other manner while we watch from the sidelines in anguish.

Remember Abraham? As he drew the knife up into the air prior to driving it into his son's heart, do you think he was remembering his prayers for God's will in his son's life?

Here is one final prayer blueprint: "Father, please help me to accept and follow willingly Your plan for my life. Help me to accept it even when I don't like it, knowing that what's happening is the best thing that can happen to me. Help me to leave my friends and my parents now that they are getting older, and do your bidding in Zimbabwe, or Pakistan, or Baghdad, or wherever else You send me. Help me to go, knowing that I'm giving up my pension and responding without knowing where my next week's paycheque will come from."

Scary, isn't it? But wait, there's more! Are you prepared to make yourself vulnerable within the family of God by openly soliciting prayer support for problems at work, a recalcitrant teenager, a family dispute or an irate neighbour? Am I prepared for this? It may be scary, but when we start praying in this fashion, it won't be long before we start seeing answers to prayer.

A number of years ago, I had the urge to try something different, which resulted in a six-month working stint in Riyadh, Saudi Arabia. There are no publicly available Christian churches there, only clandestine home churches with attendance by invitation only. Meeting with other believers was a precious experience, with corporate prayer being of the utmost importance. Much of our prayer time was spent upholding one another before the Lord. In short prayers, the congregation would review each person's needs and concerns. One would pray, and then another and another, each mentioning someone else's problems. Want to see the church grow? Start confessing your individual problems to the family, and then pray as a group for each person. That, I believe, is biblical prayer.

Many people consider that God is real. He does indeed exist to them, and He may even have created this world, but they have relegated Him to the ethereal regions. He is supernatural and reigns in a supernatural world. He is "way up there," not really involved down here at all. In other words, God is real but He's not relevant. As we discovered in the previous chapter, Heaven, the place where God dwells, is as close as a whispered prayer. By praying as He did, Jesus placed God right smack in the middle of your neighbourhood today. "Thy will be done" puts Him in charge and reminds us of that very important fact.

All of the above is a very roundabout way of saying that I'm placing myself in God's hands. With these words, I liberate myself from what others think and am free to communicate freely with the Father.

Years ago, I spent several summers as a councillor at a boy's camp. Each week of camp ran from Saturday to Saturday. At lunchtime—during a leaders' huddle that had been called to determine what activities would be suitable to pursue, considering it was our third successive day of nonstop rain—a fellow councillor stood up and quite simply prayed for the rain to stop. He prayed knowing that the regional forecast was for constant rain for the next several days. He prayed knowing the need for warm weather to enable waterfront activities, and the need for dry weather to enable crafts, games, and skills training, programmes that would cause enthusiasm in the boys and create a favourable environment to explain their Creator and Saviour to them. While he was praying, the rain was beating on the roof. For the rest of the week it rained, every day, everywhere in the county except for two miles around the camp. Us, we got rain all right. It rained every single night, but only after campfire! My fellow councillor prayed in God's will, and he believed.

The words Daniel spoke to the king are indicative of the position that we should adopt in prayer. He spoke with the calm assurance of one who resides in God's will: "Your Majesty, my God can keep these lions from devouring me. I know that He can do that, but if He chooses not to He is still God and I will still obey Him."

One final thought: notice that Jesus puts the authority of God on earth as equal to the authority He holds in Heaven. We know this intellectually, but we don't let it dominate our thinking on a practical level. As hard as that is to comprehend, we need to take it one step further. That same authority is ours. We are members of His family. When we speak from the position of God's will, we speak with all the authority of the heavenly realm. Here on earth, we are His ambassadors.

Something to think about!

Chapter 26

The Christmas Wish List

Star light, star bright
The first star I see tonight;
I wish I may, I wish I might,
Have the wish I wish tonight.

Give us this day our daily bread.

—Matthew 6:11

WITHOUT A DOUBT, THIS HAS GOT TO BE THE MOST CONTROVERSIAL VERSE for Christians in the whole of Matthew's gospel. It also represents the portion of prayer wherein we spend most of our time, yet it's only one short phrase.

In the previous chapter, we took a long look at the words "Thy kingdom come," determining that one of the most difficult tasks a Christian must accomplish, if he or she is to realise all the joy that can come from being part of God's family, is to allow God free reign. It's no accident that the petition section of prayer comes immediately after this surrender: "Lord, take control in my life now. Here are the things I am missing to do a proper job for you."

Before pursuing that thought, though, take a look at the assurance God gives us regarding all those petitions. It's found in Matthew 7:7–12, but I'm only going to quote one verse:

If you then, being evil, know how to give good gifts to your children,
how much more will your Father who is in heaven give good things to
those who ask Him!

—Matthew 7:11

That one verse says it all.

Many of our petitions result from anxiety: "Lord, keep me safe
on this trip. Lord, help me get through this job interview." Indeed, I
suspect that the two most frequently occurring verbs in our prayers
are "keep" and "need."

Now turn back a few pages in your Bible and read Matthew 6:25–
34. According to 6:32, being anxious for things only demonstrates a
lack of faith, whilst according to verse 6:34, all the worries in the world
won't solve a single problem. Instead, God has said that He will supply our needs. This doesn't mean that we should never ask Him for
things, though. There are so many references in Scripture that say
otherwise that making such a statement is pure folly. We just don't
need to take up valuable prayer time belabouring the issue. Instead,
we should be spending those moments pursuing what Scripture refers
to as the Kingdom of God.

Faith

"You don't have it because you don't have enough faith."

"Just ask God. If you have enough faith, He will give it to you."

Comments such as this can absolutely shatter a young believer's
faith, yet they appear to be the same expressions used in the New
Testament. That's hardly surprising, since they are. Satan is a cunning
old devil. If he wasn't, there wouldn't be nearly as much misery on this
earth. He knows that one of the best ways to destroy our satisfaction
with life is to interfere with our talks with God. His allies, unwitting-
ly perhaps, include those who try to encourage young believers to
challenge their faith, ask God for something, and watch their prayers
come true. Under their tutelage, people ask God for what they believe are their hearts' desires. "Hi, Lord. I really believe that You can
heal my sister/brother/mother/etc. I have faith, Lord. Show us Your

power." Maybe you've heard a prayer like that, or even prayed one yourself. Such a prayer is focused inward, on personal desires, with the petitioner placing neither God nor their own well-being into the equation. Didn't think of that, did you? Sometimes you ask and don't receive simply because it's bad for you.

When God fails to respond with the anticipated largesse, such leaders may suggest that the petitioner pray again, citing a lack of faith as the probable cause. A second "no" and our now discouraged neophyte may turn away, perhaps never to experience the depths of joy that a connected prayer life can bring.

Further to that, consider this: not every Christian has the good fortune to be born into our relatively affluent Western society. Globally, many Christians must struggle day to day just to get enough to eat. I suspect you will agree with me that a Christian born into a poor home, or in a country with low average income, is not somehow lacking in faith because he hasn't attained all the wonderful things that I enjoy.

The issue therefore becomes one of defining the nature of my need. God has promised to supply our needs. When these words were spoken, the world had no knowledge of the requirements of twenty-first-century man. TV, radio, automobiles, and electric dishwashers were two thousand years into the future. Living requirements were significantly more basic, but still there was poverty, starvation, forced labour, and slavery. Christians lived in poverty and slavery. In fact, the book of Philemon was written to request forgiveness for a slave, Onesimus. One would think that having freedom, enough to eat, clothes, one's health, and a reasonably decent place to live would all be part of our basic living needs, yet some very good Christians (including Paul and even Christ Himself) lacked some or all of these. Obviously then, needs aren't necessarily connected with our physical requirements or desires.

Our needs are those things we require to live successfully as full-fledged citizens of the Kingdom of Heaven, and to accomplish the tasks Christ Jesus has laid out for us. These needs may or may not include a physical component, but they most certainly have a spiritual one.

With that, let's get back to our exploration of the Lord's Prayer.

If you finally take the plunge and put Him in charge, there is one thing I guarantee is going to happen. Sometime in the near future,

God will ask you to do something you cannot do. You will not have the skills, you will lack the knowledge, or you will be asset-deficient. Don't believe that you are being set up to fail when this happens. To the contrary: you are being set up to succeed beyond your wildest imagination. Your inability to perform this task will leave you with only two choices: either admit failure or enter into the tabernacle of prayer and lay it all out on the table for Him to resolve. Simply stated, "let go and let God."

Action

Prayer is a call to action and a declaration of involvement. Each of us is a part of the body of Christ. Just as with the individual parts of a human body, each of us has a distinct function; if a single part is removed, the rest of the body will suffer. The parts are interdependent.

I admit, though, that some parts are better-looking than others. Here is a simple, perhaps silly metaphor that illustrates this co-dependency. Your finger is throbbing. Your eyes look down at your hand and spot a hangnail. Looking at it and wishing it to heal won't make it better. Instead, the collective body parts must decide on an action (involving the mind), go to the bathroom vanity drawer and remove the scissors (involving the feet, legs, hands, and fingers), and then trim away the offending tissue. It's a team effort. The Scripture reference is 1 Corinthians 12:12–17—especially 12:17.

Do you recall the person in Scripture who, when he saw that his neighbour was hungry, bid him be well and be filled? With that thought in mind, here's a prayer for daily bread.

> Father, Samuel is going to California to further his studies in Your Word. He's seeking to serve You and is going there on faith that You will provide. Provide for him and his family so that Your will may be done in their lives.

Good prayer? But let me change it just a little.

Father, Samuel is going to California to further his studies in Your Word. He's seeking to serve You and is going there on faith that You will provide. *Show me how I can help* provide for him and his family so that Your will may be done in their lives.

By adding just six words, it has gone from an ethereal feel-good to a dynamic action prayer. The prayer now inserts the petitioner into the solution.

Here's an example of another common prayer.

Father, I have a need for a new _____ so as to do such-and-such for You. I really need it, Lord, to do this effectively, and I know that You can provide it. But if You don't, I will understand that it isn't Your will for me. Your will be done.

So what's wrong with this picture? It has gone from being a prayer of authority to a prayer with a built-in escape clause. It provides God with a reason not to respond and to enable me to comfortably respond to someone's question about my failure to receive. All I have to do is say, "It wasn't God's will."

Friend, God doesn't need our escape clauses. Our prayers up to this point have been focussed upon Him. He is in charge, and our goal should be placing ourselves in His will. What He wants to hear from us is some indication that we have confidence that He will provide.

Father, my old Volvo has just about had it. The brakes are shot, the engine is losing oil, and the body has more holes in it than an Election Day promise. Would You see that I get a replacement? I saw one down at the dealer's place yesterday that will meet our needs. It is €10,000 over what I have or can scrape up.

Would I pray that prayer? Would you?

A few years back, I heard a young chap talking about the work he was doing in Spain. The prayer quoted above was part of his story. His work involved ministering in a number of rural mountain villages. A reliable vehicle was essential if he was going to be an effective witness. He had managed to gather together only five thousand euros, one-fifth of the sum required.

As he was working in his office, an individual stopped in to talk. The upshot of that conversation saw the transfer of 2,500 euros from the missionary's wallet to the individual who had an urgent need. The new car had become even less obtainable. But he had committed the need for a car to God and put the responsibility for its acquisition in God's hands. It wasn't long before sufficient moneys arrived from overseas to enable him to complete the purchase.

Quite simply, he wasn't hesitant about asking; he was praying from the security of knowing he was walking in God's will. In the meantime, someone back home responded as a result of his own prayers: "Father, for some reason I'm really concerned about the mission we're sponsoring in Spain. How can I best help?"

Are the things I pray for the things I need to make my life more comfortable, or are they things I need to do the job He has asked me to do?

While in prayer, it's necessary to think back to when we were praying for God's will. This is when our assignments are handed out— when He outlines the little bit He wants us to accomplish. Without knowing our assignment, it is impossible to know what we lack. These missing bits constitute our needs, which He has promised to supply. At least, that's the way I see it. What do you think?

Something to think about!

Chapter 27

Forgive Us Our Trespasses (Debts)

THERE ARE AT LEAST AS MANY DIFFERENT EXPLANATIONS OF THIS PHRASE AS there are gondolas in Venice. All are plausible. What follows is a short description of each of the most common notions. They are not written in any particular order. Consider each. Perhaps all are valid and we need to pray through each as we talk to the Father about those less than honourable moments in our lives.

Quite frankly, my early teachings about this portion of the Lord's Prayer just didn't sit right. For as long as I can recall, I was taught that we must be right with God before He will listen to us, yet here in the Lord's Prayer, reconciliation doesn't occur until the midway point. Either God hasn't listened to a word that's been spoken up until this point (explaining very nicely why so many folks never get their Christmas wish list) or the earlier teaching I received was wrong.

At one point, I was taught that confession should be an ongoing thing. That is, when I realise that I've sinned, I should immediately go into confession mode and ask for forgiveness. I suspect that's sound advice, but is that really what this line in the Lord's Prayer is all about? Before trying to answer that question, let's work through the problem of reconciliation.

Paul told the Corinthians that they were God's temple and that the Spirit of God lived in them. Therefore, according to Paul, they were holy. Read about it in 1 Corinthians 3:16–17. Now, turn to Romans 8:

Therefore, there is now no condemnation *for those who are in Christ Jesus, because through Christ Jesus the law of the Spirit who gives life has set you* free from the law of sin *and death. For what the law was powerless to do because it was weakened by the flesh, God did by sending his own Son in the likeness of sinful flesh to be a sin offering. And so he condemned sin in the flesh, in order that the righteous requirement of the law might be fully met in us, who do not live according to the flesh but according to the Spirit.*

—Romans 8:1–4, NIV (emphasis added)

I emphasized a couple of points, but the entire section is full of encouragement. Jesus, through His death and resurrection, cancelled out any debt due the devil for sins committed by any individual who calls Him Lord. The debt is paid in full, now and forever. Confession then isn't there for us to re-establish our membership in the family of God. The prodigal son never stopped being a member of his family. All he had to do was remember that he was part of the family.

When our own children do something wrong, it is generally very obvious. Their heads hang down and they won't look us in the eyes. When we pull a no-no, our reaction is much the same as our children's. Our confession simply allows us to lift up our heads in God's presence. We are the root cause of the breakdown in communication. God can always hear us and talk to us, but our embarrassment keeps us from breaking the wall of silence. We are forgiven permanently, so we do not require any further action to be taken regarding forgiveness to enter into God's throne room.

Scripture and history are in total agreement: Jesus died. The purpose for His death was to provide the human race with the gift of eternal life to all who confess their sins to Him and declare that He is Lord. In Canada, as in most countries, when an immigrant takes the oath of citizenship he/she becomes a permanent Canadian, unconditionally. Likewise, our confession of sin and declaration of His lordship makes us citizens of the Kingdom of Heaven, permanently and unconditionally. No further action on our part is necessary to reaffirm our status. A second confession is not required and in fact demonstrates a lack of faith in the completeness of His work in our lives. God therefore does not require confession before He will listen to us.

Sin diminishes our feeling of worthiness. Satan tries to ensure that the guilt we feel is magnified to the point where we feel that we are excommunicated from God, that God refuses to talk to us until we make a full confession, when in fact it is we who are refusing to talk to Him. Confused? Turn to Isaiah 6. God has called the prophet Isaiah into His presence. Isaiah declares himself unworthy to be there. A seraphim brings a live coal from the altar, touches Isaiah's lips, and then says, *"Behold, this has touched your lips; your iniquity is taken away, and your sin purged"* (Isaiah 6:7, NKJV).

Isaiah was in the presence of God in the holiest of holies at God's invitation. God therefore had decided that Isaiah was worthy to be there. The purging was not a precondition for admittance but was done in response to Isaiah's own feelings of unworthiness. So, too, it is with us. God sees us through the prism of His Son's sacrifice, so we are worthy. Do we need to confess as a condition for being heard? I would say no, but that is a personal decision.

Many of the newer translations of Scripture translate the word trespass as "debt." It's true that we owe God big-time, but it's a debt we cannot ever pay back. Christ paid the price, so asking Him to forgive our debt seems illogical. When you think about it, asking forgiveness for the debt I owe Christ is the antithesis of the request I should be making: "Lord, remind me daily of the debt I owe you, the one I can never repay, so that I may always be reminded of your great love for me (whilst I was yet a sinner Christ died for me)."

Instead, it seems that the King James Version may have come closer to the intent than our more contemporary versions. Scripture tells us that the New Testament is a continuation of the Old Testament, and lo and behold, "trespass offerings" are detailed in Leviticus 5. It's worthwhile to spend a few minutes reading it to fully understand the concept. Very briefly, a trespass offering was intended to compensate for those wrong actions we take in innocence, not realising they are indeed wrong. It was also intended as a sacrifice for our careless words that inadvertently hurt others. So, if I am reading this correctly, I'm asking God's forgiveness for having so-called normal human reactions that fail to live up to God's perfect standard.

From 1 Corinthians, we know that our sins are permanently forgiven. If that is the case, asking for forgiveness as we sin is unnecessary. As a thought, could it be that this petition is more of a request of God that He bring those hidden, forgotten, or inadvertent errors to our attention, enabling us to make corrections to our speech, lifestyle, or relationships with others so as to more closely align ourselves with Christ Himself? I certainly can't say so definitively, but I leave it with you to decide for yourselves.

As We Forgive

Jesus set the example and Stephen, Peter, and Bréboeuf (amongst others) have shown us how to have the same attitude, but "Father, forgive them" has got to be the three hardest words to say in the entire English language. It's unlikely that any of you will be placed in the position of asking God to forgive the person throwing literal stones at you, but what about the boss who passes you by at promotion time for someone less capable but whose last name is the same as the one on the letterhead? What about the neighbour who ridicules your faith or the parents who stand idly by as their children tease yours? There may be a time when you will be fired or disciplined at work and be totally innocent.

Truth to tell, I don't want God to forgive people who offend me. At least, not right away. I want them to suffer. Maybe burning in hell is a little drastic, but there's nothing wrong with a little scorching—except that there is. The full meaning of the language could easily have been lost with time, but here is one paraphrase that satisfies the intent of the original language. The prayer states, "Father, forgive my trespasses to the same degree or in the same manner as I forgive those who offend me." Or, to sort of use the Golden Rule: "Father, do unto me as I do unto others."

As you may recall, prayer isn't some mystical incantation but an intelligent conversation between yourself and God, and our sample prayer is located practically dead centre in the Sermon on the Mount, Scripture's longest transcript of Christ's teachings. The Sermon is a single cohesive lesson describing the best way to get along with others here on earth as a citizen of the Kingdom of Heaven.

Matthew 6 flows from Matthew 5 and is all about our relationship with God. The Lord's Prayer is simply a guideline to help channel our thoughts as we engage Him in conversation. Matthew 5 is all about getting along with people. So where am I going with this? This portion of the prayer is perhaps about getting us to ask God to assist us in our relationships with others.

This may be contrary to our normal perception, but it has the advantage of fitting in with the general flow of ideas in Christ's sermon. It's as though we are praying, "In my relationship with others, Lord, I am certain that there are times when I have inadvertently offended or hurt those people around me (trespass sins). Bring these offences to my attention, Lord, so as to enable me to set things right with them. At the same time, my friend said some very hurtful things about me today. Help me to forgive him and set things right."

I believe Jesus did not intend to supply us with a pat, easily memorized script. The invitation to talk with God is not one that should be taken lightly. I suspect He is less than satisfied with our perfunctory efforts. Since there isn't a single explanation for this phrase, it seems most likely that the above are all correct. Asking forgiveness within a family or business, or with God, serves the same purpose: it clears the air and improves relationships. It sets things right.

Something to think about!

Chapter 28

Lead Me Not

FIRST AND FOREMOST, GOD DOESN'T SET UP TRIP WIRES OF WRONG CHOICES, dangle the possibility of an extramarital dalliance in front of our eyes, then stand behind a bar pouring double Caesars for us to imbibe or provide us free tickets to the latest X-rated movie. God is not, cannot, and will not associate Himself with evil, nor will He endeavour to sucker us into pursuing evil on our own. So why does the Lord's Prayer suggest that He does?

It doesn't. What it says is that He leads us. With the exception of two identical phrases, this one in Matthew 6 and the other in Luke 11, there is no place in Scripture that connects temptation, God, and us.

Several of the commentaries I use suggest that God sets up situations in which we are tested in order to grow our faith, but this scenario implies that God is somehow in cahoots with Satan, since we know that Satan is the author of all evil. Instead, just as with Job, I believe God prevents Satan from initiating much of the evil of which he is capable. God pointed out to Satan that His man, Job, was of prime integrity. Satan replied that of course he was; God had put a wall around him that he, Satan, was unable to breach.

> *Have You not made a hedge around him, around his household, and around all that he has on every side?*
>
> —Job 1:10

God responded to Satan's complaint by removing some of the bulwarks surrounding Job, but Satan still had limitations upon the actions he could take.

So it is with us. God knows and understands us. It is quite likely that Satan has a similar conversation with God about every one of us, and for each of us God allows Satan to go only so far and no farther. Further, God specifically states that the leash on Satan allows him to go only so far. He cannot test us beyond our abilities, and God always provides a way of escape.

During the centuries from the departure of the Roman legions from England until the reign of Charles II of England, one notable feature of the British and Scottish landscape was the castle. Oliver Cromwell expended a considerable amount of gunpowder to eliminate many of them as places of sanctuary during the civil war. These ranged in size from a simple frontier keep to the massive royal palaces such as at Edinburgh or Stirling. Besides the massive walls, the architects took advantage of geographical features such as cliffs or islands to add additional layers of defence.

A castle was built for one of two purposes: to protect a family or to exact control over a particular feature, such as a trade route through a mountain pass or a navigable waterway. The former is easily defended by building on the top of the cliffs, but what about the waterway? In several cases, fortifications were constructed upon an island that was connected or serviced from the mainland via a bridge (easily removed during troubles), a ferry, or a carefully concealed causeway that twisted and turned back upon itself in a number of ways before finally arriving at the main gate. Only the most trusted of servants were allowed to learn the secrets of the underwater route; visitors were escorted to the island blindfolded or via boat.

The path our lives follow is much like that causeway. We cannot see a safe way through the maze, but the Lord can and does. Psalm 23 is quite specific: He leads me beside calm waters. Even though death confronts me, I don't need to be afraid because He is with me.

Then, of course, there are the words to the old hymn "He Leadeth Me." I have only reproduced one verse and the chorus, but take note of the words. He doesn't take chances with our wandering; if we let Him, He will hold our hand and guide us step by step through the pitfalls Satan has prepared. He will not lead us into temptation but will choose a route that keeps us clear.

Sometimes 'mid scenes of deepest gloom,
Sometimes where Eden's bowers bloom,
By waters still, o'er troubled sea,
Still 'tis His hand that leadeth me.

He leadeth me, He leadeth me,
By His own hand He leadeth me;
His faithful foll'wer I would be,
For by His hand He leadeth me.[8]

To summarize, Satan has all kinds of plans that he would dearly love to put in place for our discomfiture, but he's restricted by God to those events He, God, knows we can withstand. In addition, God prepares an exit path that provides a way of escape. He is standing by to take us by the hand and lead us step by step through the maze Satan has prepared, keeping each step safe.

These phrases in the Lord's Prayer are there as an acknowledgement of these facts. There are troubles that have been prepared, and the Lord is there to guide us. They are a plea for that guidance. God will never abandon us. That is His promise.

Be strong and of good courage, do not fear nor be afraid of them; for the Lord your God, He is the One who goes with you. He will not leave you nor forsake you.

—Deuteronomy 31:6

Let your conduct be without covetousness; be content with such things as you have. For He Himself has said, "I will never leave you nor

---

8 "He Leadeth Me," Joseph H. Gilmore (1862).

forsake you." So we may boldly say: "The Lord is my helper; I will not fear. What can man do to me?"

—Hebrews 13:5–6

But God doesn't give us the help we need unless we ask Him to do so. At that Scottish castle I mentioned, all were free to attempt to find their way to the gate through the bogs and marshes. But only the foolhardy would attempt to find his way independently when it was known that one misstep could lead to death.

There is one more thing to observe about the castle. The people entrusted with guiding strangers along the paths were highly trusted. The castle lord literally placed his life and that of his family in these people's hands. If an enemy were to learn the safe way through, it wouldn't be long before the castle was stormed and captured. At the same time, those seeking passage through the maze were blindfolded. They had no way of knowing the location of the next steppingstone. If they cast off the hand of their guide and removed the blindfold, what good would it do? Even though they could see their destination and their starting point, they had no way of determining a safe route forward or back.

In our prayers and in our lives, we are the same way. We know our destination, and perhaps it is visible on the horizon, but we cannot know what lies between our goal and ourselves. Yet we often cast off God's hand and set off on our own. This phrase then is a request for God to keep leading us by the hand.

No one in their right mind actively seeks out their own death, although sports such as white-water kayaking, cliff-diving, and rock-climbing do cause one to question the sanity of the individuals participating. Nevertheless, only a fool commits to these sports without taking elementary precautions such as safety lines, pitons, life jackets, and checking the water for hidden rocks and logs.

So it is in our prayer life. When talking to God, part of our prayer should include talking about the road ahead. There may be problems we can identify, so part of our conversation should include asking to avoid them. Jesus did just that in the garden before He went to His death: His prayer—"Father, can we not find another solution?" fits right in. Asking God to take us around danger, or on a path that avoids it, is only sensible.

Here's a simple example:

Father, lead me by the hand and guide my tongue as I talk to Bob about the parties his son has been throwing when left alone. Talking with him, or even calling in the tenant board, seems to be the only solution. If it is possible, can we find another way to resolve this dispute with my neighbours?

Deliver Us from Evil

Some commentators suggest that this expression should be written as "Deliver us from the Evil One." And why not? Satan is both the Evil One and the root of all evil, so the two phrases are practically synonymous. Regardless of the precautions we take, there is going to come a time when we find ourselves caught up in one of Satan's plots. It can't be avoided.

In the example of the man with the neighbour dispute, he is confronted with a problem that's not of his own making. The neighbour's teenage son starts drinking with his friends and becomes loud, crude, and obnoxious the moment his parents go out the door. Situations like this are tailor-made for community conflict. Satan would love to use this troubled teen to drive a wedge between our hero and Bob, negating any positive witnessing that may have been present before.

Then there is the boss who wants you to push your hours just a bit as a flight attendant, pilot, or truck driver. What about road rage, when you want to give the driver who just cut you off the bird or a blast of the air horn?

Lord, Deliver Me from the Evil One

The Lord's Prayer is an integral part of the Sermon on the Mount, so perhaps it's time to remind ourselves what the sermon is about. It's all about living so *"that your joy may be full"* (John 15:11). It was never intended to be a thesis on the hereafter, but a blueprint for the here and now. Jesus is talking to normal citizens caught up in the anxieties of everyday life. He is not a guest lecturer at a seminary or delivering a speech to the Commonwealth Club. His listeners were people He had healed, their relatives, and their friends. They were farmers, fishermen, craftsmen, police officials (peace makers), and yes, there were a few Bible students and church leaders present as well. Most of these folks were not terribly interested in long-term goals. They were too concerned with tonight's supper, the kids' progress at school, and balancing the books so as to meet their tax obligations. Jesus knew that it was much easier to plan a budget to keep your house warm in winter than it was to save for a three-year-old child's college education. It's likely that He worked as a craftsman to support His family up until the time He started His ministry. His teaching was practical; it had to be, or His audience would have deserted Him after the first fifteen minutes. These were practical people who could ill-afford to take an hour off work, let alone the several days that seem to have been required to come and listen to Him on this occasion.

You may hear of people spending an hour or two in prayer each day and wonder at what appears to be a misuse of time. Isn't it better to tackle those daily problems than toss them up into the ether and hope for a divine solution? In fact, the opposite is true. Prayer is practical and a worthwhile use of time. A practical reward is promised to result from each portion of the prayer. For example, the introduction produces confidence, and the hallowing of God's name produces peace and wonder. The Christmas wish list identifies those material goods we require to do the things God wants us to do, and it sets the process in motion whereby we will obtain those necessities. The current portion identifies areas of possible confrontation and passes control of those areas over to God.

When I read the local news, I'm not reading about problems in some distant province or country but rather problems over in the next block. There is very real potential for those problems to involve myself or members of my family. It's great to know that someone much stronger and wiser than I am is running interference and will show me the way to avoid the Evil One. Talking potential problems over with God before they occur, presenting Him with the names of those folks I'm having difficulty with in order to enter into a more profitable relationship with them, and asking the Father's help in escaping a debilitating habit are all wise and worthwhile uses of time. At least, that's the way I see it. What do you think?

Something to think about!

Chapter 29

For Thine Is the Kingdom

For thine is the kingdom, and the power, and the glory, for ever. Amen.
—Matthew 6:13, KJV

YOU WILL NOT FIND THESE WORDS WRITTEN IN THE CATHOLIC BIBLE. NOR can they be found in the Vulgate or in the Old Latin text. They do occur in a number of early manuscripts, maybe even a majority, including several from the second century. So what do we do? Do we drop the phrase as being irrelevant, or do we pursue it in the same manner as we have all the previous phrases?

Does it make a difference one way or the other? The New Testament is a compilation of writings from a number of authors all penned prior to 150 A.D., and probably all written much sooner than that. They present to us the words and life of Christ as presented by several eyewitnesses and three of the early church leaders (Luke, Paul, and Mark). At various times, other manuscripts have been incorporated into the biblical canon but are now excluded for various reasons. It is an absolute certainty that all of the manuscripts available to the early church leaders were carefully scrutinised prior to being accepted or rejected. Interestingly, the books contained within the Eastern Orthodox, Roman, Protestant, and Armenian Old Testaments vary, but there is almost universal agreement with regards to those in the New Testament.

The addition of these words was considered to be a triumph for the reformation church, not just because of their becoming a symbol of the reformation's rebellion against Rome but because they were visible proof of the existence of new translations from original manuscripts in the language of the believer.

That is the historical background. It's interesting (to some), but it doesn't leave us any closer to deciding whether to include these words in our prayer or not. Hopefully, one or two of you are asking yourself why I'm going on about something so insignificant. And that's the point! Prayer is not the recitation of a bunch of words found in the book of Matthew, even though they were indeed spoken by Christ Himself. Instead, prayer is an intelligent discussion between Almighty God and us. The Lord's Prayer was never intended to be our prayer. Absolutely not! Its purpose is to provide a guide to enable our minds to organise our words.

These words introduce the concluding portion of prayer. If you wish to end abruptly with a simple "That's all for now, Lord, amen," then that's perfectly acceptable. However, for those who are feeling just a little more eloquent or don't quite know how to stop, I will take a few minutes to explore the possible background to these final words.

One commentary I visited used the word "doxology" to describe the conclusion. Since the only time I can recall hearing the word was in reference to the chorus "Praise God from Whom All Blessings Flow," which our Baptist church used every Sunday morning to close out the service, I decided that it was time to visit Webster. There I discovered that a doxology is defined as "a short formula of praise to God." Not a bad explanation, I suppose, but considering this conclusion simply as a doxology really limits what the New Testament writer was trying to convey about prayer.

Doesn't it seem a little peculiar to you, if it is indeed simply a doxology, that Christ gave us a formula for prayer that concluded with giving Him a pat on the back and saying what a wonderful God He is? That just doesn't fit in with the character of God as portrayed in Scripture and as evidenced by His life on earth. Christ's life was a humble one. When cornered at His trial, He didn't say a word in his own defence. Doxology is too simple an explanation.

Starting prayer with praise is necessary to get us in the proper frame of mind. It assures us that everything is in its proper place and that God is able. After all, He is God, and therefore He can and will deliver on each of His promises—a comforting thought when our prayers consist of pleas and cries for help, as many of them do. So, although the praise is focussed on God, its purpose is to comfort us.

Let us apply the same thought line to the ending.

We have just concluded our pleas for help, our wish list, and our confessional. The conversation has caused us to look inward, and possibly created a little bit of hopelessness; some of our problems have been going on for a long time, and some of the obstacles seem insurmountable. The friend you have been praying for is still sick, and we are still waiting for that dear relative to join us in the family of God.

We have also confronted the potential for temptation and conflict with the Evil One. Even though, in the back of our minds, we know that God is right here with us, we still feel a little fearful and overwhelmed. Christ knew all about the emotions involved in prayer. After all, He was the one who sweated blood in the garden on the night He was betrayed.

Regardless of the difficulty you find yourself in—or maybe you're just winding up your daily talk with the Lord—the words "For thine is the kingdom" should provide immediate comfort. They serve as a reminder to me that I am not in control, but more importantly, neither is Satan, for I am no longer a citizen of this world.

One of the gripes one hears from American ex-pats concerns the IRS requirement that they continue to file a tax return in the U.S. But in return for this, each American travels with the assurance that their government will endeavour to come to their assistance if they need it. Over the years, there have been numerous instances of marines in full combat gear escorting terrified civilians out of holiday adventures that have suddenly become a little too exciting.

God is standing by. "I will never leave you or abandon you," He says, "because you are My subject and part of My family."

So the first words of this closing are there to provide us with reassurance regarding our security. I am a citizen of Heaven and my Lord's army is standing by to help keep me out of trouble.

The next few words were spoken to assure us that a relationship with God is more than a collection of feel-good philosophies. As you pray, recollecting these words, think of the conversation between

Moses and Pharaoh—and what happened next. By the time Moses returned to Egypt, he had been away for forty years. Nevertheless, it is quite conceivable that he had grown up with or helped in the teaching of the man who occupied the Egyptian throne. After exchanging pleasantries and getting caught up on the events that had transpired over the last forty years, Pharaoh finally asked Moses to explain what had brought him back to the court. I can imagine Pharaoh's laughter when Moses told him that he was to order the release of the tens of thousands of Jewish slaves. I doubt if there was a single major Egyptian family or business enterprise that didn't keep at least a couple of Jews. The removal of such a large labour force would have had a devastating effect on the economy, and the courts knew it.

After the laughter had subsided, Pharaoh asked Moses to explain (probably before he was thrown into jail) just where he came up with the notion that the Egyptians would entertain such a preposterous suggestion. Remember Moses' answer? "I AM has sent me to give you this message." This preceded the first of ten progressively severe miracles and plagues until finally the Egyptians paid the Jews their personal gold and silver to leave.

"I AM has sent me." That's the power that lies behind your prayer. The resources we are calling upon are far greater than those of the rulers of the earth.

Take a moment and look up Romans 8. Here are just a couple of the verses, but the entire chapter is worth committing to memory:

> *What then shall we say to these things? If God is for us, who can be against us? He who did not spare His own Son, but delivered Him up for us all, how shall He not with Him also freely give us all things? Who shall bring a charge against God's elect? It is God who justifies.*
> —Romans 8:31–33

That's some power we have to draw upon. Only the last three words of the conclusion actually invoke praise. As is evident, the majority of the expressions are aimed at assuring the petitioner that God is there, that God is listening, and that God has the legal authority, will, and tools with which to resolve the problems brought before Him.

Finally, though, there is an expression of praise towards God, although maybe it isn't so much praise as a promise and a reminder. The use of "glory" implies that I am going to give God the credit for His responses to my petitions. It's a promise from me to God.

It's possible that Christ placed these words as the final expression of His sample prayer as a reminder that it is He who performs miracles and answers prayer. We would do well to remember that simple fact.

There is one New Testament miracle in particular that emphasises this thought. Ten lepers pleaded with Jesus to be healed, but only two came back to say thanks. We should say, "Lord, when things go well and people pat me on the shoulder, saying what a great job I've done, help me to remember to give you the credit, forever and ever. Amen."

Those last words are self-explanatory. God is the same today and forever, and His promises are valid for the same length of time. The words pack a lot of meaning, far more than a simple expression of praise. Were they spoken by Christ? The answer will have to wait until we get to Heaven, but you have to close a prayer in some fashion, and I can't think of a better way than by recognizing His sovereignty, power, authority, and right to respond to my requests—and conversely, Satan's lack of authority over me. The words of praise with which I conclude my prayer are there to remind me to give God the credit rather than to give God a pat on the back.

Something to think about!

Chapter 30

The Preposition Matters

A PREPOSITION IS A WORD EXPRESSING THE RELATIONSHIP BETWEEN A NOUN, a pronoun, or a noun phrase that immediately follows the preposition called the object and another element of the sentence. Different meanings or applications for the same word can be achieved simply by varying the preposition.

Now, that may seem like a strange way to start a look at prayer, but getting the right preposition in our minds may mean the difference between getting answers to prayer and wondering why there never seems to be any dialogue between oneself and our Creator.

With that as an introduction, I pray that I've piqued your interest enough to keep reading.

I can remember a sermon on prayer in which the minister made reference to the simple fact that God always answers prayers. There are three answers that He gives: yes, no, and not yet. Another minister further defined "yes" by suggesting that God would either provide the exact solution we had proposed or an even better solution, based upon His infinite knowledge of what's best for us. Other pastors have suggested that prayer is talking things over with God until we reach the point where we agree with whatever is going to happen anyway. This is the "Thy will be done" philosophy.

Do they all sound familiar? These solutions seem grossly inadequate. They tend to suggest that there are limits on prayer, and limits on what God will do in response to prayer. Yet as we saw in the last chapter, prayer is omnipotent. It can do anything that God can do. So why doesn't it?

This is where the preposition comes in. In Isaiah 40:31, we read, *"Those who wait on the Lord shall renew their strength."* The word "wait" means simply to remain in a place or in a state of inactivity, indecision, delay, or anticipation because of some event expected to happen or some person expected to arrive. It generally appears with the preposition "for". Waiting is a common pastime in Brussels—for the tram, the bus, the metro, a friend, or (my favourite) one's paycheque. In Scripture the phrase "wait for" is often negative (for example, describing an army waiting in ambush). Its positive applications are most frequently in regards to God's promises:

> *And being assembled together with them, He commanded them not to depart from Jerusalem, but to* wait for *the Promise of the Father, "which," He said, "you have heard from Me."*
> —Acts 1:4 (emphasis added)

Generally speaking, waiting is a real drag and we tire of it quickly. When waiting for the tram, sixty seconds can seem like as many minutes, particularly when it's raining or cold. It's also unproductive time. Now change the preposition to "on" and see the difference:

> Wait on *the Lord, and keep his way, and he shall exalt thee to inherit the land: when the wicked are cut off, thou shalt see it.*
> —Psalm 37:34, KJV (emphasis added)

> *Say not thou, I will recompense evil; but wait on the Lord, and he shall save thee.*
> —Proverbs 20:22, KJV (emphasis added)

"Wait on" and "wait for" have different meanings. In medieval times, the king would have a number of equerries who were constantly with the monarch to attend to any tasks he or she might require. A butler also fits this job description: a person who attends to the needs and requirements of his employer and is in constant attendance upon him. When paraphrased, Isaiah 40:31 becomes: "A person who remains in the presence of the Lord will renew his strength." Psalm 37:34 becomes: "If you remain in attendance upon the Lord and do things the way He wants them done, then He will exalt you and you will inherit the land. You will live to see the wicked cut off."

"Wait for" implies that the event or person for whom you are waiting isn't there yet. It is a future event. Every answer to prayer isn't going to come instantaneously, although some do, so what becomes important is what we're doing whilst waiting.

In Niagara, the local Sears office is strictly a package delivery facility. Sears will telephone when my order is in, at which time I go to the office with my claims slip and ask for my package. While I wait at the counter, the clerk goes back into the warehouse, locates the package, and brings it forward to the front desk. If I don't wait for the package at the counter, I will never receive it. Instead, it will be sent back to the central warehouse with an "UNABLE TO DELIVER" stamp on the outside.

How many prayers and petitions are sent up using the Charlie-Brown-wish-upon-a-star method? After delivering the list to God for processing, we blithely turn around and go about our business whilst waiting for God to deliver on our requests. And we wonder why there don't seem to be any answers! I wonder how many answers to prayer have been brought forward to the counter by God only to find that we haven't bothered to hang around to hear or receive the answer.

Contrast the two references below. Isaiah 59:9 produces a feeling of despair:

> *Therefore is judgment far from us, neither doth justice overtake us: we wait for light, but behold obscurity; for brightness, but we walk in darkness!* (KJV)

Now look at Lamentations:

The Lord is good to those who wait for Him, to the soul who seeks Him. *It is good that one should hope* and *wait quietly for the salvation of the Lord.*

—Lamentations 3:25–26 (emphasis added)

The bottom line is that whilst we're waiting for answers, we should be waiting on God. It's that simple. God answers prayer. God delivers on His promises when we're there to listen to the answer and accept delivery. Every reference regarding waiting in Scripture emphasises this simple truth.

For evildoers shall be cut off; but those who wait on *the Lord, they shall inherit the earth.*

—Psalm 37:9 (emphasis added)

Behold, as the eyes of servants look unto the hand of their masters, and as the eyes of a maiden unto the hand of her mistress; so our eyes wait upon *the Lord our God, until that he have mercy upon us.*

—Psalm 123:2, KJV (emphasis added)

And I will wait on *the Lord, who hides His face from the house of Jacob; and I will hope in Him.*

—Isaiah 8:17 (emphasis added)

But those who wait on *the Lord shall renew their strength; they shall mount up with wings like eagles, they shall run and not be weary, they shall walk and not faint.*

—Isaiah 40:31 (emphasis added)

Wait on *the Lord; be of good courage, and He shall strengthen your heart;* wait, *I say,* on *the Lord!*

—Psalm 27:14 (emphasis added)

Wait on *the Lord, and keep His way, and He shall exalt you to inherit the land; when the wicked are cut off, you shall see it.*

—Psalm 37:34 (emphasis added)

Do not say, "I will recompense evil"; wait for the Lord, and He will save you.

—Proverbs 20:22 (emphasis added)

Something to think about!

Chapter 31

Even Pastors Make Mistakes

Dear Pastor,

The wife and I were talking in the car on the way home last Sunday about the way things are going at the church. She said, and I agree, that she thought she saw a lot of good, healthy growth amongst the regulars. Brother Dave asked me on the way out if I could teach a Young Adults class for the next little while, as his class is just too big. It seems that when new folks in the neighbourhood stop in on a Sunday, they just keep on coming.

Your sermons have gotta have a lot to do with that, Pastor. They just keep on getting better and better. Like that series you just finished on prayer. I never realised that my prayers had so much of an impact in Heaven. You really think I can change God's plans simply by praying? That's amazing!

Anyway, the reason I'm writing is to ask if you could lend me that book by Blackaby that you used last summer. Dave left it open as the materiel to be used and I thought it would provide a good foundation for the new folks in the church. If it's okay with you, I'll pick it up at the church sometime later this week. Thanks in advance,

Sincerely yours,

Third Pew Back, Left-Hand Side.

Dear Third Pew,

I do appreciate your words of encouragement, and of course you are quite welcome to borrow the book. I will leave it with Ethel in the front office so you can pick it up whenever you like.

It is grand to see the pews full and to know that the folks sitting in them are eager to hear what the Word says. I can't imagine a more rewarding place to be than right here and right now. But if your words are any indication as to the lessons learned regarding prayer, I can see that I am going to have to give at least one more sermon on the subject in the not-too-distant future.

It isn't about anything that you got wrong. Instead, it's about something you got exactly right. If that sounds a little enigmatic, don't worry. It was intended. If you're in the third pew on the left, come Sunday morning you will hear a full explanation.

Sincerely yours,
The Pastor

* * *

I do hope that I've created enough of a mystery. Have you detected any errors in our friend Third Pew's writings? The pastor said that what he had written was correct, so what has caused the need for his changing his planned sermon?

Third Pew expressed his wonder that God not only heard his prayers but would make changes to his plans in response to them. Upon reading Third Pew's letter, the pastor realized that he had committed a grievous error, the same one this writer has made. What is the error? Read on.

God has a plan for our lives. That plan promises the very best for us, provided we stick with the plan.

In Genesis 12:2, God made a promise to Abram. Abram was going to be the founder of a great nation. At the time of the promise, Abram was seventy-five years old. For the next ten years, Abram and his with Sarai waited for God's promise to come true. They grew weary of waiting and finally Sarai gave her handmaiden to Abram. Nine months later, Ishmael, the father of the Arabic tribes, was born. It was another dozen years before Isaac was born. When that occurred, Sarai insisted that Ishmael and his mother be driven out of the family homestead, and there has been division between the two family lines ever since. Just think: the ongoing wars between Israel and the Palestinians are a direct result of Abram and Sarai trying to provide their own solution to God's promise. It's true that Ishmael was probably not an answer to prayer; regardless, the ongoing saga of Isaac and Ishmael is an excellent example of the problems we can get into when we don't stick with the plan.

By anybody's standard, Moses was an exceptional man. He is the only person in all of history to have seen God's glory. God was his friend! When God first gave Moses his assignment to lead the Israelites out of Egypt, Moses provided God with every excuse in the book as to why he was an unsatisfactory selection. His final rationalization concerned his inability to speak. Moses dug his heels in on this very point. God relented and told him that he would commission Aaron, Moses' brother, as his spokesperson, but that Moses would retain overall command. Thus Aaron was God's compromise with Moses.

In Exodus 24, Moses appoints Aaron as acting leader of the people of Israel. In Exodus 32, we find that it is Aaron's mind that decides upon a golden image as a substitute for God, and it is Aaron's hands that craft the final product. It was Aaron, in his role as priest, who led the people in worshipping the calf and sacrificing to it.

Numbers 12 records the attempt by Aaron and his sister Miriam to increase their own stature in the community by belittling Moses. It seems that Aaron wasn't as sincere in his beliefs as his brother. I suspect that he enjoyed the perks of leadership but he doesn't appear to have had any deep convictions of his own. Witness his leading the people in idol worship. Perhaps it would have been better for both he and the people if Moses had just accepted the assignment of leadership as given by God.

Hezekiah had been a good king. He had torn down the temples that his predecessors had built to various local gods, demolished their altars, and re-established the worship of Jehovah. He was both a good leader and a righteous man, and perhaps because of that God sent him word via the prophet Isaiah that it was time to put his affairs in order, because the illness he had developed was fatal.

Here are the events as recorded in Isaiah:

"Thus says the Lord: 'Set your house in order, for you shall die and not live.'"

    Then Hezekiah turned his face toward the wall, and prayed to the Lord, and said, "Remember now, O Lord, I pray, how I have walked before You in truth and with a loyal heart, and have done what is good in Your sight." And Hezekiah wept bitterly.

    And the word of the Lord came to Isaiah, saying, "Go and tell Hezekiah, 'Thus says the Lord, the God of David your father: "I have heard your prayer, I have seen your tears; surely I will add to your days fifteen years. I will deliver you and this city from the hand of the king of Assyria, and I will defend this city."'"

—Isaiah 38:1–6

Because of his faithfulness, God honoured his prayer and added fifteen years to his life. Shortly after Hezekiah's recovery, he received a royal delegation from Babylon. Perhaps as an attempt to show that Israel wasn't just a dusty backwater on the road between Damascus and Alexandria, Hezekiah showed his guests the contents of the royal treasury. After fifteen years, Hezekiah died and his son Manasseh became king.

Here is what 2 Kings has to say about Manasseh:

And he did evil in the sight of the Lord, according to the abominations of the nations whom the Lord had cast out before the children of Israel. For he rebuilt the high places which Hezekiah his father had destroyed; he raised up altars for Baal, and made a wooden image, as Ahab king of Israel had done; and he worshiped all the host of heaven and served them. He also built altars in the house of the Lord, of which the Lord had said, "In Jerusalem I will put My name." And he built altars for all the host of heaven in the two courts of the house of the Lord. Also he made his son pass through the fire, practiced soothsaying, used witchcraft, and consulted spiritists and mediums. He did much evil in the sight of the Lord, to provoke Him to anger. He even set a carved image of Asherah that he had made, in the house of which the Lord had said to David and to Solomon his son, "In this house and in Jerusalem, which I have chosen out of all the tribes of Israel, I will put My name forever.

—2 Kings 21:2–7

There is nothing good to be said about Manasseh. Israel had been on its way to becoming the light on the hill that God had wanted it to be under Hezekiah. Manasseh ended that. But what has that to do with Hezekiah's prayer? Manasseh was only twelve years old when his father died and he was crowned. If Hezekiah's prayer had not been answered, Manasseh would never have been born and Israel's future might have been significantly different. It's also possible that Babylon would never have invaded if Hezekiah hadn't shown off the royal treasures. After all, why expend money and lives on capturing a fortress city (Jerusalem) unless there are known rewards to collect? God sent Isaiah to the king after his show-and-tell session and told him that Babylon would conquer Jerusalem as a direct result of his boasting. Perhaps Hezekiah should have accepted God's original plan for him.

It is evident from these examples that God will sometimes (not always) change His plans as a direct result of our intervention. It is also evident that those changes may not be in our own best interests. Does this mean we should never ask for changes? Certainly not! But we do need to ensure that we put God's plan first in our lives and be certain that what we are requesting is in line with that plan, even if it means our lives are shortened by fifteen years.

Something to think about!

Chapter 32

Have You Seen Any Good Miracles Lately?

MIRACLES ARE AMAZING JUST FOR THE FACT THAT THEY ARE MIRACLES. They are generally unexpected, beyond explanation, and fly in the face of logic. They just shouldn't happen. But then again, if they were planned, explainable, and logical, they wouldn't really be miracles, would they?

A miracle is, by definition, a supernatural event brought about through divine intervention. Or, for those events people don't wish to attribute to God, a miracle is any event that defies the odds in its occurrence. For example, "It was a miracle he wasn't killed when the avalanche buried his cottage in five meters of snow."

I truly suspect that we encounter miracles far more frequently than we admit. In fact, I suspect scarcely a day goes by that our lives aren't graced by some form of miracle. So why aren't we absolutely bursting to tell our friends and family about God's latest intervention in our lives? Perhaps it's because we are always looking for the spectacular, and in so doing we miss the everyday, ho-hum, run-of-the-mill miracle that's occurring right underneath our proboscis.

Elijah the prophet didn't have an easy time of it. He was the guy who had to tell Jezebel and Ahab that God wasn't pleased with them, at a time when those two were actively trying to eliminate any trace of Judaism in Israel. Avoiding a fatal encounter with those two put Elijah right at the centre of some pretty spectacular miracles. He was fed by ravens, outran a horse, and called down fire from heaven. He even called upon God to restore a dead lad to his mother and dined on a single loaf of bread and jug of wine for three years.

Remember the story? Elijah had challenged the 450 priests of Baal to a duel which ended with fire being brought down from Heaven onto Elijah's altar and his leading the people of Israel in the subsequent slaughter of all Baal's priests. Immediately after these events, Elijah, anointed with God's Spirit, ran back to town, arriving ahead of a mounted king Ahab. I'm certain you will agree with me when I say that Elijah was a man who knew miracles. But when Jezebel threatened him later that same day, he fled into the desert and there asked God to end it all for him. He was tired, discouraged, and alone.

He stayed there for a day and a night, and during that time an angel fed him a stone-baked cake that provided him with sufficient nourishment to sustain him for what ended up to be forty days of wandering. From where he was to where he went is about two hundred miles, so he could have done it in just a little over two weeks, yet it took closer to six. There was no indication that God was leading him; he was just wandering with no direction or purpose.

Upon arriving at Mount Horeb, the mountain of God, he immediately slunk into a cave from which he was finally aroused by a voice basically telling him to get off his butt.

> *Then He said, "Go out, and stand on the mountain before the Lord."*
> *And behold, the Lord passed by, and a great and strong wind tore into*
> *the mountains and broke the rocks in pieces before the Lord, but the*
> *Lord was not in the wind; and after the wind an earthquake, but the*
> *Lord was not in the earthquake; and after the earthquake a fire, but*
> *the Lord was not in the fire; and after the fire a still small voice. So it*
> *was, when Elijah heard it, that he wrapped his face in his mantle and*
> *went out and stood in the entrance of the cave. Suddenly a voice came*
> *to him, and said, "What are you doing here, Elijah?"*
> —1 Kings 19:11–13

Poor old Elijah! Just like Jonah (and we all know how that turned out), he had been trying to run away from God. True, he had done everything God had asked him to do, and in so doing he had been part of those amazing events recounted earlier—and true, the wicked Jezebel had threatened him with immediate death—but these facts don't cancel out the inescapable truth that Elijah was trying to flee from God.

Perhaps Elijah thought about God and His miracles in much the same way we do. As long as we are doing His will and He has a job for us to do, we feel that we're basically bulletproof: "Satan can try, but he can't seriously touch me because I am doing God's work." When we start thinking this way, we start considering God as the God of the big picture, the God who choreographs the big event. But God isn't that way at all. And so He called Elijah out of his hole with an invitation to meet Him.

So, where was God? He wasn't in the wind or the earthquake or the fire. These were mighty events that caught Elijah's attention, for sure. Indeed, even a cynic would be hard-pressed to deny that these occurrences were miraculous, but they didn't signal the presence of God. But then came the voice, and Elijah realized, perhaps for the first time, that all these miracles he had witnessed—indeed, that he had initiated—were simply tools of God. They weren't God! God is not confined to the supernatural, and miracles do not provide us with the definition of God.

God is intimately personal and at the same time Lord of the universe. God speaks to us, He cares for us, and yes, sometimes He intervenes in the natural process of things to answer us when we call out to Him in pain, frustration, and disillusionment. For Elijah, the revelation was simply that *God is*. It's the same lesson Moses was taught when he encountered God. Remember?

> *And God said to Moses, "I AM WHO I AM." And He said, "Thus you shall say to the children of Israel, 'I AM has sent me to you.'"*
> —Exodus 3:14

He cared for Elijah not because He still had work for Elijah to do, but simply because He cared for Elijah.

Now, let's go back to the definition of the word miracle. According to Webster, a miracle is "a supernatural event brought about through divine intervention." From Elijah's experience, I would propose a change: "a miracle is any event brought about through divine intervention." Without that change in definition, we run the distinct risk of missing out on God's presence in our lives, just as Elijah did.

A young lady once sat in a church pew, with friends and family close by, yet she was still very much alone. In grief, she pondered her future and cried out to God in despair, "What now?" For the last several years, her entire purpose in life had been to care for her mother as she struggled through the pain of ultimately futile cancer treatments. She was at her mother's funeral service, and she was now alone at twenty-seven. She didn't regret the past several years. As a child, her mother had been her best friend, always supportive and always ready with a comforting arm about the shoulders. It had been difficult, yet an honour, to care for her mother. Now it was over

What now, indeed? There just didn't seem to be anything worthwhile in the future. Both her siblings had spouses to share the grief and help one another through this time of healing, but she, who had borne the brunt of the care over the last several months, had no one, and no one even noticed.

Traffic noises suddenly became louder as the church door opened; they were then muted as the door slammed closed. She heard footsteps coming up the aisle and a frustrated-looking young man sat down right next to her in the family pew. He bowed his head and folded his hands in an attitude of prayer.

The man's eyes showed evidence of tears as he apologised for being late, although he did not supply any explanation. After several different friends of the woman's mother had paid tribute, he leaned over and quietly asked her why they were referring to her as Margaret instead of Mary.

"That was her name," the woman replied. "No one ever called her Mary."

At this point, she was wishing he had sat anywhere but beside her. Why was he in the family section anyway? She had never seen him before.

"No, that isn't correct," he insisted. Several people glanced over at them. "Her name is Mary. Mary Peters."

"That isn't who this service is for."

"Isn't this the Lutheran church?"

"No, the Lutheran church is across the street."

"Oh."

"I believe you're at the wrong funeral, sir."

The death of her mother, the funeral trappings, the organ playing mournfully contrasted with the man's obvious mistake. She burst out laughing, shaking with the effort to suppress it and earning glares of rebuke from those around her.

As soon as the service ended, she and the stranger left quickly. He invited her to share a coffee with him as partial compensation for disturbing her grief.

You can see where this is going, can't you? Yes, the coffee led to dinner and eventually the two were married. That mistake was the start of a lifelong journey together, and they now have the perfect explanation as to how they met. Her mother and his Aunt Mary introduced them. It was a match made in heaven.

God had answered her cry before she had even uttered it, and in a better way than she could ever have imagined. There was no hurricane-force wind, no bone-rattling earthquake, and definitely no raging fire. There was only a still small voice. What's your definition of a miracle?

Something to think about!

Chapter 32

Arachnophobia

AFTER AN EXHAUSTIVE SEARCH THROUGH SCRIPTURE, I HAVE DETERMINED that there are no references to spiders anywhere. Not one! Nada. So why would any devotional bear a title about something that isn't there?

Lots of people hate spiders, and I do admit that there are lots of things not to like about them. They are definitely not the most beautiful creation; I'm thinking of tarantulas in particular. Anyone who has walked into a spiderweb can attest to the crawly feeling those sticky strands can give.

Spiders are not insects but arthropods: a family made up of three main groups, arachnids, insects, and crustaceans. Not all spiders spin webs, but all produce silk threads that are used to spin a cocoon around their eggs. Instead of a web, the bola spider uses a strand of silk capped with a blob of "glue" as a type of lasso. When it detects a potential meal coming within range, it will swing the strand in an arc, intending to intercept the unsuspecting prey in flight. Anyone who has watched what happens to a dog when it runs out to the end of its rope for the first time knows exactly what happens next.

The spider maintains a hold on the thrown strand, causing the tagged insect to halt abruptly in flight. Bola spiders prefer moths as a main delicacy and even give off a species-specific moth-like odour to further attract them. But if moths aren't available, they will lasso any manageable insect that comes along.

A second intriguing species of spider is the water or diving bell spider. This air-breathing creature spends its life almost entirely immersed in water. Both male and female water spiders spin an underwater bell of silk that they anchor to the stems and leaves of plants. The female's bell is larger, as it provides both a home for her and a nursery for the eggs she lays within a cocoon that she spins at the top of her diving bell. The body of these spiders is covered with very fine hairs that trap air in bubbles during the occasional trip to the surface. Insect larvae provide their main diet. The bell has tripwires of silk suspended from its frame. The water spider is alerted when a passing larvae brushes against one of these lines. The design of the bell permits them to exit quickly and pounce without losing any of their precious air supply. Interestingly, perhaps because of its dual function as home and nursery, the female must make the occasional trip to the surface for air, whilst the male remains almost entirely submerged. In water that is sufficiently oxygenated, these trips to the surface become unnecessary as the design of the bell permits

> *gas exchange with the surrounding water; there is net diffusion of oxygen into the bell and net diffusion of carbon dioxide out. This process is driven by differences in partial pressure. The production of carbon dioxide and use of oxygen by the spider maintains the concentration gradient, required for diffusion.*[9]

These are just two species of many that use silk for purposes other than making a web. One spider species is even vegetarian. Fancy that.

The species that catch our attention most are the orb-weaving spiders. These are the chaps that spin those beautiful webs between branches. But how does a creature that can't fly manage to bridge the large gaps that webs regularly span? The process is fascinating. A fine line with a dab of glue on one end is carefully released into the air. Air currents carry it along until it makes contact with a solid object. When the spider detects the change in tension, it carefully pulls in the line until it's taut and ties it off. Treading carefully, as the first line is extremely light, the spider makes its way across to the other side, laying a re-enforcing line beside the first line as it goes.

---

9 *Wikipedia*, "Diving bell spider." Date of access: February 26, 2015 (http://en.wikipedia.org/wiki/Diving_bell_spider).

Weaving a web is not a simple process. Although it appears as though the spider is producing a single strand at a time, it may in fact have between two and eight spinnerets to use together (producing a thick, heavy strand of silk) or independently. A spinneret is the organ that produces the silk strands, which incidentally start off as a liquid that congeals quickly upon exposure to air. What appears at first glance to be a simple nozzle is in fact composed of a multitude of microscopic spigots, each producing one filament. Thus a single strand is in actuality a multiple microscopic filament of silk. Multiple strands provide a much stronger result than would a single strand of the same diameter. So we have multiple nozzles within a spinneret, and up to eight spinnerets to work with as well. This flexibility permits spiders to combine multiple filaments in different ways to produce many kinds of silk for special purposes.

A spider can construct a normal-sized orb web in just a couple of hours. Speed is of importance because the glue loses its glueyness in just a couple of days. When this occurs, the spider will eat its own web, recycling all of the materials, and spin a new one.

For us humans, the closest comparable artistry we demonstrate comes from Flanders: lace. Since medieval times, artisans there have been creating this most beautiful and intricate product. Originally the skill was passed from mother to daughter, but cultural changes in the twentieth century broke this family tradition in many homes, and machines churning out simple lace patterns reduced the demand. Ironically in some respects, this reduction in demand has increased the value of the work—and skilled lace makers are never without work. A lace maker may spend a month or more on a single intricate design whilst a large project such as a dress or tablecloth may take several lace makers eight or nine months to complete.

No one is born with the knowledge necessary to produce fine lace. It takes years of work before a lace maker masters the art, starting with just a few bobbins and gradually adding complexity until she's comfortable working with one hundred or more. She learns by watching her mentor at work and then copying the mentor's actions under close supervision, anticipating the day when the pattern upon which she's working is considered of sufficient quality to be offered for sale.

Artists develop new lace patterns through trial and error, drawing the concept out, trying it out, and then making corrections until they're satisfied with the end result.

The orb-weaving spider is considered to be the oldest variety. By what process would an orb-weaver evolve into a bola spider? Let us suppose for a moment that sometime in the distant past an orb-weaving spider, in endeavouring to connect that first fine strand, accidentally snared a passing moth and did so every time she tried to make a web. Her success enabled her to live a full life with lots of children and grandchildren clustering around in her old age, but she died without ever completing a web, becoming, by accident, the world's first bola Spider. Whilst this type of success would certainly be reason enough to patent a new technique in our own world, for spiders there is unfortunately no process by which they can pass on this learnt skill.

The only way an orb-weaving spider could become a bola spider is for there to have occurred a change in programming, requiring some form of genetic change. Even this brief description of the workings of a spinneret should show the potential complexity of the change required—and remember, the spider's dinner depends upon the change working successfully the first time and every time.

When we see a piece of lace, we are unanimous in our praise of its intricacy and beauty and the artistic genius of its creator. When we see a freshly spun web silhouetted in the early morning sun, we are again unanimous in our praise of its intricacy and beauty. What a beautiful device for catching flies! So why do we not acknowledge the Creator who conceived of and caused the spider to exist simply through His word?

I will leave you with a few verses from Psalm 104. Perhaps when you have a minute this evening, you might take the time to read the complete chapter.

What You give them they gather in; You open Your hand, they are filled with good. You hide Your face, they are troubled; You take away their breath, they die and return to their dust. You send forth Your

Spirit, they are created; and You renew the face of the earth... Bless the Lord, O my soul! Praise the Lord!

—Psalm 104:28–30, 35

Something to think about!

Chapter 34

This Church Will Self-Destruct in...

DO YOU LIKE THE TITLE? I THOUGHT IT WAS RATHER CATCHY, SO EVEN THOUGH my thoughts have changed completely and are no longer as advertised, I decided to leave it.

This week started off in Isaiah and has ended up in Matthew—in particular, Matthew 13. Here are the particular verses that caught my eye. I have included both the parable and Christ's explanation.

Another parable He put forth to them, saying: "The kingdom of heaven is like a man who sowed good seed in his field; but while men slept, his enemy came and sowed tares among the wheat and went his way. But when the grain had sprouted and produced a crop, then the tares also appeared.

"So the servants of the owner came and said to him, 'Sir, did you not sow good seed in your field? How then does it have tares?'

"He said to them, 'An enemy has done this.'

"The servants said to him, 'Do you want us then to go and gather them up?'

"But he said, 'No, lest while you gather up the tares you also uproot the wheat with them. Let both grow together until the harvest, and at the time of harvest I will say to the reapers, "First gather together the tares and bind them in bundles to burn them, but gather the wheat into my barn."'"

Another parable He put forth to them, saying: "The kingdom of heaven is like a mustard seed, which a man took and sowed in his field, which indeed is the least of all the seeds; but when it is grown it is greater than the herbs and becomes a tree, so that the birds of the air come and nest in its branches."

Another parable He spoke to them: "The kingdom of heaven is like leaven, which a woman took and hid in three measures of meal till it was all leavened."

All these things Jesus spoke to the multitude in parables; and without a parable He did not speak to them, that it might be fulfilled which was spoken by the prophet, saying: "I will open My mouth in parables; I will utter things kept secret from the foundation of the world."

Then Jesus sent the multitude away and went into the house. And His disciples came to Him, saying, "Explain to us the parable of the tares of the field."

He answered and said to them: "He who sows the good seed is the Son of Man. The field is the world, the good seeds are the sons of the kingdom, but the tares are the sons of the wicked one. The enemy who sowed them is the devil, the harvest is the end of the age, and the reapers are the angels. Therefore as the tares are gathered and burned in the fire, so it will be at the end of this age. The Son of Man will send out His angels, and they will gather out of His kingdom all things that offend, and those who practice lawlessness, and will cast them into the furnace of fire. There will be wailing and gnashing of teeth. Then the righteous will shine forth as the sun in the kingdom of their Father. He who has ears to hear, let him hear!"

I'm certain that you have read this parable before, as well as the explanation, but please carry on reading. Hopefully you will discover something a little new and different as a result, as I did.

In the explanation, Jesus omits identifying two particular groups. He identifies Himself as the sower, Satan as Satan, and the angels as the reapers, but He doesn't identify the men who were sleeping. The second unidentified group are the servants who were seeking to put things right. Any guesses?

Notice, please, that there is no attempt on the owner of the field's part to find fault with those who were sleeping. The parable refers to farmers, not soldiers, and there was no requirement for a farmer to post sentries to keep out trespassers. Instead we are given a picture of a normal, tranquil agricultural community. The people were going about their normal duties, and in the course of time they went to sleep. Obviously the enemy was watching, and as soon as things were quiet he availed himself of the opportunity to stealthily sow some weeds.

Christ identifies the field as the entire world. Commentators generally suggest that this refers to the church, since Christ is talking about the Kingdom of Heaven. Certainly the good seed sown should be linked to His followers, as He labels them "sons of the kingdom," but perhaps we need to go back a little further in time to get the whole picture.

A farmer who wants to obtain the best possible crop spends as much time preparing the soil to receive the seed as he does in the later harvesting process, and this applies to all crops. The text implies that the field referred to in Matthew was weed-free when the wheat seed was planted. We can assume this because the owner states that the tares were introduced by an antagonist and were not there to begin with. Achieving a weed-free condition requires leaving the field dormant for at least a single growing season, during which time the farmer ploughs it on a regular basis, turning the weeds to permit the summer sun to scorch their roots and prevent them from going to seed. The ploughed field is then harrowed to uproot any remaining weeds, which are dragged to one side. The field is tilled one more time to break open the soil and permit the seed to penetrate the surface just prior to seeding. It's a lot of work. Scripture states that Christ started this soil preparation "before time began."

In hope of eternal life which God, who cannot lie, promised before time began...

—Titus 1:2

God promised Adam that He would provide a Saviour. There were only eight people on earth following the flood. All eight had been witnesses to the catastrophic destruction of almost all life, and they were active participants in the rescue of those fortunate enough to survive, yet within only a few generations God was forced to pronounce judgement once again at the site of Babel. There were people alive in Babel who had known at least the grandsons of Noah, but it was to no avail. Life for most was good; those few parents who declared allegiance to God were considered to be out of touch with the times. A tower was the way to get closer to God (according to the kids), and Satan crept in to sow his weeds while the majority of concerned citizens slept.

If Noah's kin had remembered the lessons of the flood, they would have listened for God, and none of us would have to learn French or English or Swahili in order to be understood, but no one ever opens their eyes to the problems going on around them until disaster strikes. I'll bet the most common prayer heard in Heaven is "God, if you will... I promise to..."

The promise of a Saviour was also made to Noah, Abraham, Moses, the judges, and the prophets. Christ's birth was the most predicted event to ever occur. There should have been thousands of people crowding around the stable in Bethlehem as soon as Joseph and Mary rode into town. Everyone from the high priest to King Herod should have been there.

It was two years before several eastern mystics sent Jerusalem's heads spinning with rumours that the Messiah had been born. His birth was the beginning of the final tilling of the field in preparation for His crop, the sons of the kingdom.

When the seed started to germinate, His servants were aghast. "You planted good seed," they cried. "What happened?" Commentaries suggest that these servants were church leaders, but it seems more likely that these true servants of God were, in fact, angels. They had seen His sacrifice, witnessed His torture and death, and then saw all His work seemingly choked out by weeds. "We'll take care of it, master," they said.

If we take their words literally, and the context doesn't give us any reason to do otherwise, we discover that these servants are suggesting the total removal of the tares from the field—or, to translate, the death of all those whose lives are under Satan's control. But Christ forbids it.

There's no way to remove the weeds from a wheat field without destroying a significant portion of the crop. In our modern era, it would be possible to spray for weeds using an aircraft, but certainly this was not the case in biblical times. Weeding was done by hand and by hoe. Walking through a field of young wheat causes the stalks to break, whilst an individual wielding a hoe cannot be selective enough; his efforts will root out wheat as well as weeds.

Through the parable, Christ explains to his disciples why the kingdom can't happen immediately, and why sin will seemingly thrive in the meantime. It's something for us to remember, too. Whenever we see people suffer, or when we hear our God being blasphemed by government leaders, teachers, and neighbours, we're apt to question whether God is indeed in control. God's patience regarding His creation is questioned frequently throughout Scripture. Psalm 74 is just one example of many:

> *They said in their hearts, "Let us destroy them altogether." They have burned up all the meeting places of God in the land. We do not see our signs; there is no longer any prophet; nor is there any among us who knows how long. O God, how long will the adversary reproach? Will the enemy blaspheme Your name forever? Why do You withdraw Your hand, even Your right hand? Take it out of Your bosom and destroy them. For God is my King from of old, working salvation in the midst of the earth.*
>
> —Psalm 78:8–12

Christ flatly forbade His servants from passing sentence upon those people who were not His followers. Every individual, regardless of his attitude towards Christ, is entitled to his full season in the sun.

The clear message is: leave the weeds alone until harvest. People's lives are inextricably interwoven. As believers, we can cause significant spiritual damage if we isolate ourselves, or heartily condemn any who we believe are not worthy of our association. It isn't up to us to pass judgment.

Perhaps Peter was thinking of this parable when he wrote his second letter:

> *But, beloved, do not forget this one thing, that with the Lord one day is as a thousand years, and a thousand years as one day. The Lord*

is not slack concerning His promise, as some count slackness, but is longsuffering *toward us,* not willing that any should perish but that all should come to repentance.

2 Peter 3:8–9 (emphasis added)

Something to think about!

Chapter 35

Searching for Treasure

DEAR PASTOR,

The parables in Matthew 13 have me and the wife stumped. Christ explained the first one, so we don't have a problem with that, but when we came across verse 44 we just couldn't agree, nor could either of us find a concordance that seemed to make any sense. In a couple, the authors bypassed any attempt at an explanation, instead providing a literal application of Jewish law in the finding of treasure. It was useful background information, but not much use in understanding. One said the hidden treasure symbolized the truth about Christ being buried in Scripture (the field). The accidental discovery aspect made us doubt that one. When I phoned my brother-in-law and asked him, he said the buried treasure was Christ Himself and the sinner was giving up everything he had to attain his salvation. Couldn't agree with that one; we choked up on the price tag, since salvation is supposed to be free.

When you have a moment, could you write back and give us your thoughts? It would be greatly appreciated. By the way, the wife wants to know if you and the missus would like to join us for Sunday dinner? We could maybe talk about it then.

Sincerely yours,

Third Pew Back, Left-Hand Side

Dear Third Pew,

First of all, thanks for the dinner invitation. My wife and I would be pleased to join you, but we will save the theological discussion for another time, if you don't mind. Barb is too good a cook to have her dinner go cold whilst we talk. When I did a sermon series on Matthew, I encountered the lack of consensus you mentioned. After much study, I did eventually come up with an explanation that satisfied my own position.

> *Again, the kingdom of heaven is like treasure hidden in a field, which a man found and hid; and for joy over it he goes and sells all that he has and buys that field.*
>
> —Matthew 13:44

It is only thirty-five words, and as such it ranks as one of the shortest parables in Scripture. The disciples evidently understood it, since there is no explanation given—but that was then. Now there's no agreement amongst Bible scholars.

Most of Christ's teachings centred on thoughts regarding the Kingdom of Heaven, and this parable and its companion found in Matthew 13:45 is no exception. At first glance, the four gospels appear to consist mainly of red type (Christ's own words), but it isn't long before one realizes that we really don't have a great deal of Christ's teaching written down. Therefore, the recorded words must be of great significance: He wanted us to know them. With that as an introduction, let's get started.

The Parable

Buried treasure! The immediate image from the twenty-first century is one of faded and torn maps, a lonely desert island, and a group of unkempt prisoners digging a hole in the sand to conceal ill-gotten doubloons and gold jewellery whilst Captain Blackbeard sits on the chest with a pair of flintlock pistols trained on the unhappy labourers. The picture comes courtesy of a hundred years of Hollywood epics.

But that's not the way it was, at least not in first-century Palestine. The Royal Bank of Canada, ING, FORTIS, and the like didn't exist. Instead, burying valuables was the common way to protect them from theft. Folks would go out behind the house, find a suitable spot they could remember, and bury their cash until such time as it was required. The fact that these buried hoards sometimes turn up today is proof that people didn't always remember where to dig. Every once in a while, one of these buried savings accounts is discovered by someone out digging in their garden or some such thing. The National Geographic Daily News from June 19, 2012 featured one such stash, discovered in a residence near Megiddo. The heavily tarnished coins were pure silver. Such treasure troves are valued in the millions of dollars today, but when they were buried the value of these coins would not have been an unrealistic sum for a reasonably wealthy man to keep on hand at the time.

In the parable, it is evident that an earlier owner had concealed the treasure. After all, if the current owners had buried it, they wouldn't be selling the land without retrieving their savings first.

Along comes our hero, though, and he hasn't a clue. He doesn't know that a treasure of any kind exists. He's just moved into the neighbourhood, or maybe it's a place he has visited frequently over the years; we don't know, nor does it matter. Perhaps he kicks over a rock. There it is! Treasure! It's beautiful, it's valuable, and it doesn't belong to him. If he takes it, the owner of the property will hear of it and take steps to get it back.

Carefully he conceals any evidence that anything other than earth has been found. He ensures that the stone is put back exactly as he found it, that even his footprints are brushed out. There's too much at stake to take chances. He knows that the treasure is worth every penny he can scrape together. The price tag on the field is such that he has to dispose of everything he owns in order to make the purchase price. Finally, with the cash in hand, he goes to the current owner, makes payment, and then, according to Jewish law, both the land and the buried treasure were legally his.

The Explanation

The reason theologians cannot reach agreement is possibly because they are trying to be too complicated. As far as the disciples were concerned, there was no great mystery. They said that they understood it completely. The disciples weren't scribes or theologians, but ordinary folks like you and I. As well, they weren't gifted with extraordinary insight into Scripture, at least not at the time. As evidence, notice that they asked Jesus to explain the parable of the tares (Matthew 13:36). Therefore, the explanation behind this parable must be relatively straightforward.

The original owner of the field is God. He designed and built the place, and one of His actions was to conceal within the very fabric of the earth a treasure with a value far beyond any man's comprehension. The field could be anywhere, so in the absence of a statement to the contrary let us not attach any particular significance to it. The buried treasure signifies citizenship in the Kingdom of Heaven, as the verse intimates.

The hero of our story is not looking for a change in lifestyle. In fact, he has never paid any attention to stories about the Kingdom. Perhaps he doesn't even know it exists. Regardless, it hasn't influenced his life before this sudden discovery. The verse doesn't give any details regarding his actions leading up to his discovery, so that can't be important either. It is sufficient that a man discovered the ultimate reason for living strictly by accident.[10]

Having discovered the treasure, the man immediately covers it up again. Perhaps the reburial implies that he isn't sure whether he really wants it or not. It's something he can accept or reject. Perhaps he finds the price too steep. In the parable, though, our friend immediately disposes of all his assets in order to attain ownership of the field.

---

10 When man stands before his Creator, the one thing he won't be able to say is "I never knew." All creation stands as evidence that God *is*. Christ is the most verifiable man in history. There is more evidence to support the story of His birth, life, death, and resurrection than any other historical figure. The evidence of changed lives and the testimonies of His followers add further credence to the veracity of Christ's claims regarding the Kingdom.

Before going any further, it is advantageous to look at the companion parable:

Again, the kingdom of heaven is like a merchant seeking beautiful pearls, who, when he had found one pearl of great price, went and sold all that he had and bought it.

—Matthew 13:45–46

Once again, we have a valuable item with a price tag equal to everything the purchaser owns, but this time the purchaser is searching for the item openly. The item is readily available, albeit very costly.

By considering the two parables, we are able to eliminate some of the misunderstandings that have arisen. The second parable suggests a couple of things. First, prior knowledge is not a detriment to attaining citizenship. The Jews were God's chosen nation. They had prior knowledge of the existence of the Kingdom and its immense value. Such knowledge, though, was not synonymous with actual possession. Thus the merchant represents those Jews who were earnestly searching for the Kingdom.

The first story was used by Jesus to provide a venue for another truth: prior knowledge and specialized interests/skills are not a prerequisite for entry into the Kingdom of Heaven. Such a statement opens up the Kingdom to all residents of the planet Earth. In short, Jesus is saying that the Kingdom of Heaven is accessible to both Jew and Gentile, can be readily found by the seeker (the merchant), and all others will be made aware in some fashion whether they seek it or not.

Notice that both parables set the same price, and this is the final lesson to be learnt from these parables (at least for this go-round[11]). Both men involved are able to afford the asking price, but that price is everything that the purchaser possesses. Christians have a tendency to focus on the free gift aspect of salvation. It's true that salvation is free, but our reaction to God's gift can be nothing less than total commitment. We give out of love for Him, said love having come as a

---

11 I am absolutely certain that there are more truths contained in these two verses just awaiting another occasion.

result of the pure joy of living, which is a by-product of our salvation. But being a Christian is a lifelong commitment requiring everything we possess.

I have written enough. I will finish up with an oft-repeated quote from Jim Elliot, a man who was killed by the very group of people he was trying to bring the gospel to. He said, "He is no fool who gives what he cannot keep to gain that which he cannot lose."[12]

Hopefully these thoughts will help you and Barb draw your own conclusions regarding these parables of Jesus. God bless you and we will see you on Sunday in the third pew back, left-hand side.

Something to think about!

---

12 Elisabeth Elliot, *In the Shadow of the Almighty* (New York, NY: Harper and Row, 1949), 174.

Chapter 36

Re-capped

GO FOR A DRIVE DOWN ANY MAJOR HIGHWAY IN NORTH AMERICA AND IT won't be very long before you come across the tattered remnants of a truck tire. If you are very unlucky, it's even possible that someday you may be driving right alongside one just at the moment it decides to let go. Truck tires are inflated to three times the pressure of a normal automobile tire and support significantly more weight, so when they blow, they're both very loud and potentially very destructive. That rubber weighs a lot and it is travelling at a hundred kilometres per hour. None of these tires come from the prime mover, or tractor; they're all from the trailers. Nor does a car tire ever blow in such a fashion. Only truck trailer tires disintegrate when they blow.

In an effort to save significant quantities of cash, many operators equip their trailers with re-caps instead of purchasing new rubber. A re-cap, as its name suggests, is a worn-out tire that has been renewed by having a new tread pattern vulcanized (a heat process that literally fuses new rubber and tread onto the old). Laws prohibit the use of re-caps on the tractor, but allow their use on trailers. New tires cost more than five hundred dollars a piece, but re-caps are only half that. So on a trailer with twelve tires, a company can save a lot of money. And they're safe—that is, as long as they're maintained with the correct air pressure. If the tires aren't right up to pressure, the cap will flex or ripple along the top of the base rubber. This continuous flexing eventually will cause the seal between the tread and tire to give way, and the tread will peel right off.

Tires don't readily lose pressure. Some type of abuse, such as a puncture, driving over significant potholes or broken pavement, excessive loading, high pavement temperatures, or simply a loose valve generally precedes pressure loss. Overheating is the primary reason for failure, for when a tire gets soft, it gets hot. But whatever the reason, a simple daily inspection of the tires will ensure years of dependable service from your tires, re-cap or not.

Unfortunately, a driver doesn't always take the time to check all of those eighteen or more wheels carefully, although he's supposed to. Sometimes, even though he notices that the tread is starting to lift, he will try and push it one more trip, gambling with reasonable odds that the tire will make it through again. It sometimes takes a long time for the tire to finally let go. Or maybe his dispatcher tells him to either drive it the way it is or he will find someone else to take the load. Whatever the reason, he sets off one more time—and somewhere down the road, maybe after hitting a few ruts or having to jam on the brakes because one of those little Smart Cars cut him off, the tire lets go and our driver is left sitting on the side of the road waiting for a repair crew to show up.

Incidentally, new tires go flat too. But a new tire can take a lot more abuse and run soft for a lot longer without letting go—and they don't normally blow as violently as a re-cap will. That is because the new tire is all one piece. It isn't new rubber glued onto an old core.

One more thing about tires: it's hard to distinguish a re-cap from the genuine article without a close inspection. They are both round, black, and have a distinctive tread pattern.

In the gospels, Jesus told His disciples not to use new fabric as a patch on an old garment (Matthew 9:16), but that isn't the comparison I want to make (although I'm certain there are thoughts to be had along that line). No, the notion that crossed my mind has more to do with our own re-birth—not so much what it is, but more particularly what it is not.

Genesis 1 records the events that occurred during the six days of creation. The very last thing God created was man. This is the next thing that happened:

Then God saw everything that He had made, and indeed it was very good.

—Genesis 1:31

Our physical decline is mapped out in Scripture starting in Genesis 3. Before man's ejection from the garden, our life expectancy was limitless

Then the Lord God said, "Behold, the man has become like one of Us, to know good and evil. And now, lest he put out his hand and take also of the tree of life, and eat, and live forever"—therefore the Lord God sent him out of the garden of Eden to till the ground from which he was taken. So He drove out the man;

—Genesis 3:22–24

It would seem the adage that we grow wiser with age isn't in keeping with Scripture. Genesis makes it clear that living longer just caused us to create more mischief, and God got fed up with being patient.

And the Lord said, "My Spirit shall not strive with man forever, for he is indeed flesh; yet his days shall be one hundred and twenty years."

—Genesis 6:3

By David's age, we were down to seventy or eighty years, which is about where we sit now in spite of modern medicine, improved hygiene, physical aids (public transit instead of walking, machines for the heavy stuff) and a better diet (McFries and Timbits?). Have a look at Psalm 90!

For all our days have passed away in Your wrath; we finish our years like a sigh. The days of our lives are seventy years; and if by reason of strength they are eighty years, yet their boast is only labor and sorrow; for it is soon cut off, and we fly away.

—Psalm 90:9–10

For early man, two hundred was a young age! All the achievements of medical science in the last hundred years has only kept pace
with our physical deterioration. We just aren't what God intended,
both inside and out.

You have to believe that when God makes something, He makes
it absolutely good. God didn't make people to be re-caps. He made
us as the genuine article. Unfortunately, we are no longer direct descendants of the perfect man. Time and decay have inevitably brought
about irreparable damage to what was God's greatest creation, and
although we may have a strong physical resemblance to the original
Adam and Eve, our internal composition (DNA) contains a multitude
of errors and weaknesses. Inside modern man lies the core of what
could have been, but the outside is all re-cap.

The Bible tells the story of God reaching out to man. For whatever reason, He wants us to be with Him throughout eternity. However, our days are limited, as you can see. As we are without Christ,
we cannot possibly live a millennium, let alone eternity. In order for
the prophecies to come to pass regarding our futures, God had some
serious reconstruction to do. Re-capping our souls won't work; re-
caps can't take the stress without giving way. An entirely new spiritual
"tire" is needed instead.

> But God, who is rich in mercy, because of His great love with which
> He loved us, even when we were dead in trespasses, made us alive
> together with Christ (by grace you have been saved)...
>
> —Ephesians 2:4–5

> And you, being dead in your trespasses and the uncircumcision of your
> flesh, He has made alive together with Him, having forgiven you all
> trespasses...
>
> —Colossians 2:13

God has made a whole new inside for all of us who have asked
Him for it. He has excised the soul that was dead and replaced it with
the eternal version: the one with an unlimited warranty.

Therefore, if anyone is in Christ, he is a new creation; old things have passed away; behold, all things have become new.
—2 Corinthians 5:17 (emphasis added)

Now, back to the tires. Re-caps and new tires look the same. They also perform the same tasks. Until the very last second in its life, a re-cap will function in exactly the same manner as the new tire. But as time goes by, and the pressure fluctuates with temperature, load, highway speeds, and rough roads, the tread cap starts to flex. The bonding that attaches it to the tire base begins to give way, and little by little the tread tears away. This may happen over a period of days, weeks, or months even, but once that first tug occurs, the ending becomes inevitable.

With one final tear, the tread peels off entirely and is shot away from the still inflated tire, which remains amazingly intact. (If you could stop the tire and take the weight off completely at this precise moment, you would find that you were looking at a completely bald rubber doughnut.) This stage only lasts for a few seconds, as the heart of the re-cap, the original tire, cannot stand the road stresses without the protective cap of the tread to protect it. The tire heats up extremely rapidly and literally explodes, tearing a huge hole in the side of the tire.

You know, people are the same as those tires. Oftentimes you cannot distinguish between those who have eternal souls and those who do not. There are some really, *really* nice people who don't believe that they are damned, so it isn't possible to use niceness as a criterion for eternity.

The next time you find yourself passing an eighteen-wheeler on the highway, take a moment to look at those tires. Are they caps or are they originals? Then ask yourself this question: "Has Christ replaced my re-capped soul with the eternally guaranteed version?" Eternity depends upon your answer. And that is, indeed, something to think about!

Chapter 37

Get Out of the Boat!

And Peter answered Him and said, "Lord, if it is You, command me to come to you on the water."

—Matthew 14:28

WEBSTER TELLS ME THAT FAITH IS THE "COMPLETE ACCEPTANCE OF A TRUTH that cannot be demonstrated or proved by the process of logical thought." Well, there was no logical reason to ever believe that Peter could stand on water. He was only able to do so because Jesus told him to do it.

I'll bet that I first heard the story of Peter walking on water as a pre-schooler in Sunday school, and I know that I've referred to it a few times before when talking about faith. Yet even though I must have read the above verse a hundred times or more, I find that it still has lessons to teach me. Follow along, if you will, whilst I share the latest with you.

The most common lessons taught from this passage are regarding Peter's lack of faith. Perhaps, however, the commentators are missing a more important lesson.

In the episode related in Matthew 14, Peter steps out of the boat and walks towards Christ. During his walk, he looks down at his feet and suddenly realises that what he's doing isn't really possible: people can't walk on water. Consequently, he starts to sink. He calls out to Christ, who reaches out and helps him to climb back into the boat. The story is often used to demonstrate lack of faith, and I suppose this is one lesson that can be learnt. But as I was reading the verses the other day, another more important truth became evident.

Faith is a function of obedience. Faith isn't just believing that God will do something for you, but rather that God will do what He says He will do. Secondly, faith is believing that God will provide me with the tools to do the things He asks me to do. Before Peter got out of the boat, he looked out at Christ and said, "Tell me to, and I will." Christ told him, and he did. He got out of the boat and started walking towards Christ.

Faith is about believing God. There was no logical reason to ever believe Peter could stand on water. He was only able to do so because Jesus told him to do it.

Consider this. Scripture tells us that faith without works is dead. Here's a simple question: do you believe God? If the answer is yes, then the next question is, "Have you stepped out of the boat?" God has given each of us something to do that involves stepping out of the boat. We each have an assignment that we cannot accomplish on our own. We need Him, but we have to get out of the boat to meet Him.

Did you catch that?

We have to get out of the boat to meet Him.

Only Peter met with Jesus that day. Oh yes, the rest were there, but only Peter was blessed by the Master's touch.

Faith doesn't guarantee success, or at least not success as we would normally measure it. Isaiah is a prime example of this. I don't think anyone would deny that Isaiah was a man of faith, yet his life was totally dedicated to failure. And he knew it. His assignment from God is found in Isaiah 6:

> *And He said, "Go, and tell this people: 'Keep on hearing, but do not understand; Keep on seeing, but do not perceive.' Make the heart of this people dull, and their ears heavy, and shut their eyes; lest they see with their eyes, and hear with their ears, and understand with their heart, and return and be healed."*
>
> *Then I said, "Lord, how long?"*
>
> *And He answered: "Until the cities are laid waste and without inhabitant, the houses are without a man, the land is utterly desolate,*

the Lord has removed men far away, and the forsaken places are many
in the midst of the land."

—Isaiah 6:9–12

I don't think any pastor has ever faced such a bleak future: "Isaiah, go and tell a bunch of people who aren't going to listen, won't understand, will close their ears to the truth, and will not repent. And keep preaching this message until Israel is destroyed." You can't find success as we picture it anywhere in those orders.

Faith and failure do not belong in the same sentence. Although the church elders would probably have taken Isaiah to task for his failure to foster church growth, Isaiah was an unqualified success by God's standards. He diligently performed the tasks God set out for him and put down on paper those warnings for the future God told him about. No less an authority than Jesus Christ used Isaiah as a reference author, and his words appear numerous times as quotes by the New Testament authors.

When we step out in faith, we do so with the absolute certain knowledge that Christ *will not* allow us to fail. Peter found that out. When he looked down at his feet and forgot who had issued the orders, Christ was there to reach out and help him back on his feet. They then walked together back to the boat. Peter did not fail. He was successful in obeying Christ's orders to come to Him. Jesus made sure of that. God assures us that He will be there to provide whatever help we need to complete the faith task He has set for us:

But seek first the kingdom of God and His righteousness, and all these
things shall be added to you. Therefore do not worry about tomorrow,
for tomorrow will worry about its own things. Sufficient for the day is
its own trouble.

—Matthew 6:33–34

Being a faithful follower is hard work. The disciples had faith, and most of them ended up dying for it. Hebrews 11 recounts the major faith events in the lives of those listed. Each achieved their position on God's heroes-of-faith list for the same reason: they obeyed God. These were all heroes of God: David, Abraham, the prophets, and Jacob. But Scripture doesn't give evidence of reward for their faith. In actuality, the opposite is true. Take a moment to reread Hebrews 11.

> *These all died in faith, not having received the promises, but having seen them afar off were assured of them, embraced them and confessed that they were strangers and pilgrims on the earth. For those who say such things declare plainly that they seek a homeland. And truly if they had called to mind that country from which they had come out, they would have had opportunity to return. But now they desire a better, that is, a heavenly country. Therefore God is not ashamed to be called their God, for He has prepared a city for them.*
>
> —Hebrews 11:13–16

These folks weren't looking for rewards on earth. They were guaranteed a place in Christ's kingdom, so why would they have settled for short-term success here?

Faith, as we have seen, is setting about to do the impossible with God's help. There's nothing easy about that. In fact, it's probably the hardest thing you can set about doing. And God doesn't promise that it will get any easier as you follow along.

Prior to a battle, scouts try to pinpoint the opposing forces' strong points. Artillery units take extra care to ensure that these strong points receive special attention. A sniper knows that after he has taken his shot, the enemy will focus their fire upon the area from which they believe the shot originated. If he wishes to be around to take a second shot, it behoves the sniper to either lay low or move very quickly to a different location.

So it is with us. If we are following God's orders, it's an absolute certainty that we will come in for special attention from Satan and his minions as he seeks to destroy God's strong points. If you're seeking tangible rewards, faith is the wrong way to go about it. Take a look at the last seven verses of Hebrews 11:

> *And others were tortured, not accepting deliverance, that they might obtain a better resurrection. Still others had trial of mockings and*

scourgings, yes, and of chains and imprisonment. They were stoned, they were sawn in two, were tempted, were slain with the sword. They wandered about in sheepskins and goatskins, being destitute, afflicted, tormented—of whom the world was not worthy. They wandered in deserts and mountains, in dens and caves of the earth.

—Hebrews 11:35–38

Financial success, good health, great kids, and a beautiful home are not guaranteed, and achieving them isn't an indicator of your level of faith. Faith is believing God. Faith is demonstrated by your obedience to God. You can't meet God if you stay in the boat.

Something to think about!

Chapter 38

More from Webster

In the last chapter, we left off with Jesus rescuing Peter and then walking with him back to the boat. I would like to propose another ending.

In my imaginary version, Peter successfully walks across to where Jesus is waiting and grasps His hand, then looks back at the boat with an impish grin on his face. He had done it. Immediately, so as not to be outdone, Judas calls out, "Master, command me to come to you!" Scarcely are the words out of his mouth than Matthew asks, and then John, and then all the others. It seems like great fun, cavorting on the waves in the middle of the Sea of Galilee, soaked by rain, illuminated by successive lightning bolts, and assured in the knowledge that they are with their Lord.

Now, assuming the story unfolded as I have just suggested, would the other disciples have been demonstrating faith or trust?

Here are the two definitions, as found in Webster's:

Faith (noun): Complete acceptance of a truth that cannot be demonstrated or proved by the process of logical thought.

Trust (noun): Confidence in a person or thing because of the qualities one perceives or seems to perceive in him.

Does it matter whether the proposed aquatic exercise demonstrated faith or trust? Both are excellent qualities. Think about it for a couple of minutes!

What conclusion did you come to? There's an entire chapter dedicated to people of faith. Out of all the Bible heroes, only these few are singled out. By implication, a man of faith occupies a special place in the heart of God. All of the New Testament writers emphasise the importance of faith. We are lost without it. That's a given. Unfortunately, in our pursuit of faith, we seem to have reduced the importance of trust. We have faith in our salvation, we constantly plead with God to increase our faith, and we stand in awe of those stalwarts whom we perceive as living a life of faith. All of these are good things. There's a *but*, however, and that's what I would like to focus on today.

Do you trust your government? Assuming for the moment that you answered no, the next question of course is, why not? Do you trust your family physician? Assuming that this time the answer was yes, the next question is, why?

Let's consider the family physician first. I would suggest that your responses regarding your basis for trust are similar to my own. I trust him because when I require his diagnosis, it's generally accurate. I trust him because his training was taken at an accredited university. I trust him because he doesn't rush his diagnosis but takes the time to verify each symptom before drawing conclusions. I trust him because he takes the time to explain his actions one step at a time. I trust him because of his quiet confidence and evident knowledge.

Do those reasons match your own? I suspect there are others, but these will do for now.

It's time now for the question on government. I don't trust the government because of the financial scandals that seem to surround its members. I don't trust the government because of the way they seem to waste my tax dollars. I don't trust the government because of the way they seem to neglect the environment. I don't trust the government because... are your answers similar to mine?

When I review the two lists and compare them, the first thing I notice is the absence of first-person experience to justify my lack of trust in government. My rationale for trusting my physician is based primarily upon personal experience, whilst my reasons for distrusting government are based primarily upon news stories and suppositions.

Trust or its antithesis relies upon knowledge. By definition, trust requires our having first-hand experience with the person or subject in question. Faith, on the other hand, requires no such experiential knowledge. Because of this, faith can be misplaced. In the example above, I faithfully believe that my government is untrustworthy, yet such faith isn't justified if I make that statement based solely upon my personal knowledge and experience.

I believe that Scripture is one hundred percent truth. It is God's truths written for me. I have to accept portions of it on faith. Creation, for instance, cannot be proven scientifically, although it can certainly be justified logically. Likewise, the predicted end of this age must be accepted on faith. We won't know until it happens. I have faith that my salvation is assured as outlined in the gospels. These are all truths which can only be accepted through faith. But faith does not, nor should it be, left to stand alone.

This is where the importance of trust comes in. I have faith that these events occurred, or will occur, because I can trust the Author of Scripture. God has provided evidence. Prophecy, history, and nature provide sufficient proof that God both exists and that He has done everything that Scripture claims He has done. I can trust Him for the future because He has proven Himself to be totally trustworthy in the past. I have both the experience of others, as recorded in books and in Scripture, and I have personal experience, so I'm not relying upon second- or third-hand information. Trust, therefore, provides a reliable foundation for faith.

Trust comes from experience and/or observation. In my alternate storyline, the other disciples stepped out of the boat with the added assurance of having witnessed Peter's successful excursion. Being eyewitnesses to such a miracle would most certainly have bolstered their trust in Jesus. So, too, our trust in God is reinforced each time we witness His work around us and with each personal encounter we have with the Master.

Trust is earned. Without trust, the foundation for faith becomes mere intuition, and experience has taught me many a hard lesson regarding intuition: it's often wrong. God has demonstrated that He is trustworthy. With each experience in which I see His hand at work,

I become more confident in His leadership—so that when He sets a task in front of me that seems impossible, I can have confidence that He will help me see it through to completion.

Trust is only good up until the first time a person fails to deliver as promised. As proof of this, answer this question: would you knowingly board an aircraft with a flight crew that had been involved in an accident, even though that same flight crew had logged thousands of accident-free hours? God has put His all on the line. His book bears His name. If the contents of that book cannot be depended on to be accurate, neither can its author.

God calls on me to do things I cannot accomplish by myself. If I rely upon Him and fail, He proves Himself untrustworthy. Peter's faith was inadequate for the task of walking on water, but Jesus was right there to catch him, help him onto his feet, and walk with him back to the boat. He had proven Himself to be trustworthy and reliable.

Every time I open my Bible, attend a Bible study or home group, pray, or join together with other believers on a Sunday morning, I reinforce that knowledge, and consequently I am able to trust Him more, because trust is based upon knowing.

Faith and trust are both needed virtues. Faith believes that I can do anything God asks me to do as long as I rely upon Him for assistance. Trust believes that God will do what He says He will do.

Something to think about!

Chapter 39

Having an Affair

I RECEIVED AN INTERESTING EMAIL THIS MORNING, SO INTERESTING THAT I dropped my previous idea for this chapter. The question, asked rhetorically, was regarding adultery and why it features so strongly in Scripture. Adultery is found throughout both the Old and New Testaments. It's even part of Jesus' Sermon on the Mount. It's also one of the most common contributors to church and family breakdowns. So let's have a look at it.

Before we look into adultery, it's worthwhile to examine the relationship God intended us to have with each other.

In The Beginning

God created the Heaven, the earth, and every living and inanimate object we see today, but He saved His greatest efforts until the end. Notice the wording in the Genesis 1 passage below. God, in a conference with His Son and Spirit, decided to replicate Himself in a created being, so He made man and woman. Our relationship with our spouse was intended to be a duplication of the relationship that was enjoyed between the three components of the Godhead. He gave them authority over the earth and all of His creation and He blessed their joining together. God blesses the union between a man and woman. It happens in obedience to Him and it represents the harmony He originally envisioned when He created us in the first place.

Many scholars attribute the writing of Genesis to Moses. God provided the words spoken by Adam in Genesis 1:23 to Moses as he wrote under inspiration, but the description of the miracle of unity that follows is God's: "When you come together," He says, "you become one." The words that close a Christian wedding today—"What God has joined together let no man tear asunder"—should strike terror in people contemplating adultery. Regardless of whether you're Christian or not, marriage is God's creation and a person who meddles with it openly incurs God's wrath. Here is the marriage equation in God's plan:

$$\text{Sex} = \text{Marriage}$$

Yes, that's right. They should be one and the same.

Then God said, "Let Us make man in Our image, according to Our likeness; let them have dominion over the fish of the sea, over the birds of the air, and over the cattle, over all the earth and over every creeping thing that creeps on the earth." So God created man in His own image; in the image of God He created him; male and female He created them. Then God blessed them, and God said to them, "Be fruitful and multiply; fill the earth and subdue it; have dominion over the fish of the sea, over the birds of the air, and over every living thing that moves on the earth."

—Genesis 1:26–28

Therefore a man shall leave his father and mother and be joined to his wife, and they shall become one flesh.

—Genesis 2:24

As a matter of interest, did you take note of the words in Genesis 1:28? We were originally given authority over the earth. Yet Satan rules today.

Then the devil, taking Him up on a high mountain, showed Him all the kingdoms of the world in a moment of time. And the devil said to

Him, "All this authority I will give You, and their glory; for this has been delivered to me, and I give it to whomever I wish."

—Luke 4:5–6

We lost a lot when we gave in to temptation!

The Definition of Adultery

Adultery is a sexual relationship in which one or both parties are in a marriage relationship with another. But the word doesn't come from the same root word as our current word "adult." Instead, its root is a Latin word meaning "to alter" or "to corrupt." Simply stated, adultery seeks to alter or corrupt God's creation.

Adultery is always preceded by lust. Now, lust is not necessarily sexual in nature; it is the desire to possess. Lust is defined as

> *sinful longing; the inward sin which leads to the falling away from God (Romans 1:21). "Lust, the origin of sin, has its place in the heart, not of necessity, but because it is the centre of all moral forces and impulses and of spiritual activity." In Mark 4:19 "lusts" are objects of desire.*[13] (Easton's Illustrated Dictionary)

Lust is a selfish desire to attain something. It's an uncontrolled craving—a small-g god that we create in our own minds. Any sentence regarding a lust begins with "I want to have/get/take..." I'm sure you get the picture. Some people lust after money or prestige or power. For others, it's the desire to take what is rightfully someone else's. What greater way is there to prove your power than to take another person's spouse? We have prettied-up lust recently by employing such words as libido and sexual desire, and we justify adultery by accusing the other person of not being understanding, but in the end it comes down to wanting something that's not rightfully ours.

---

13 Easton, Matthew George. *Illustrated Bible Dictionary, Third Edition* (Nashville, TN: Thomas Nelson, 1897).

The target of lust becomes a goal, and once obtained it is a possession. It's a thing. When the target of lust is another person, the expression "RACA" could be used.[14] It is a logical progression of thought. A look at Potiphar's wife illustrates that these feelings aren't confined to the male of the species:

> *And it came to pass after these things that his master's wife cast longing eyes on Joseph, and she said, "Lie with me." ...So it was, as she spoke to Joseph day by day, that he did not heed her, to lie with her or to be with her.*
>
> —Genesis 39:7, 10

A look at Old Testament law quickly reveals that adultery (indeed, any sexual sin) was considered by God to be among the most serious crimes. The punishment for adultery was death. Jewish law was unique in that it ordered the same punishment for both man and woman.[15] The reason for this is simple: adultery destroys. It destroys the marriages involved, it destroys families, and it contributes to a breakdown in society. It contributes to child crime, abuse, alcoholism, and just about every other societal problem you wish to name. It's also destroying the church from within.

Our Greatest Need

Our greatest craving is to establish relationships. In Genesis, God gave us His plans for a healthy and fulfilled life. A fulfilled life needs people. We were not intended, ever, to be alone in this world. We need companions, and only when we establish correct relationships with them can we fully enjoy the fruits of those relationships. People know when someone is hitting on them even if nothing is ever said or done.

---

14 RACA: "Vain, empty, worthless, only found in Mat 5:22. The Jews used it as a word of contempt. It is derived from a root meaning 'to spit.'" (Matthew George Easton, *Easton's Illustrated Bible Dictionary* [Nashville, TN: Thomas Nelson, 1897]).

15 Many societies considered women to be mere possessions, so a married man could do whatever he wished with her.

It destroys their trust. But remember when reading that we're talking about present living, not future rewards.

But I say to you that whoever looks at a woman to lust for her has already committed adultery with her in his heart.

—Matthew 5:28

God made man and woman. He made them beautiful to look at. He doesn't expect us to avert our eyes every time a lady passes by (or a man, but for the sake of simplicity I will only refer to one from now on, if you don't mind). Nor, however, did He intend for us to manufacture steamy bedroom scenes with each passage. Our appreciation of beauty, our ability to discover beauty in the things around us, is God-given. Every fine feeling we possess is God-given as well. God loves beauty (see Genesis 2:9). After all, He made it, starting with the original horticultural centre, Eden. But all the beauty around us is only a fraction of the beauty of that original garden. Jesus saw and walked in the garden. After each day of creation, God looked at what He had made and saw that it was good. When God created man, He made him into His own image—so you know that it was good.

You see, Satan has taken one of God's beautiful things and tried to corrupt it in our eyes. Just like murder, adultery starts in the heart and the mind. Instead of beauty and potential love, we think of possession and satisfaction. This includes one's own spouse, by the way. Many marriages, I'm sure, end up on the rocks because people confuse sex in marriage with love. Now, if there isn't sex in marriage, you might have cause to question the depth of the love, but sex in God's vision of true love is giving, a result of love; it's not a taking, but a sharing. Read Solomon's Song. It's all about love and loving and being loved. There is plenty of implicit sex, isn't there? There are also beautifully expressed descriptions by both partners of the beauty of the other. So there is no sin in sex. We have it backwards, which is what Satan wants. Illicit sex isn't the original sin; it is the result of sin.

Something to think about!

Chapter 40

Lessons from a Broken Blender

The Story

ONE OF THE LESSONS I RECALL FROM HIGH SCHOOL COMPOSITION CLASSES concerned titles. "In order to have your material read," said the teacher, "it is necessary to create an eye-catching title to encourage the would-be reader to proceed past the first sentence." Hopefully the title above will achieve this goal. Seriously, though, the title is absolutely correct. These thoughts originated with a broken blender. It may sound silly, but it's true.

We have an old Sunbeam electric food blender. For years it has done us yeoman service, but there came a day when the blender fell off the counter and hit the floor. Although it looked okay, it wouldn't turn on; none of the speed selector buttons would even push in. Because Sandy was busy in the kitchen, the blender got stuck back in the cupboard rather than being deposited in the trash, and there it sat until yesterday. Rather than just pitching it, I decided to try and identify the problem—so into the shop it went. Step one was to remove the bottom screws.

What that revealed was a cluster of wires leading into a switch panel, and of course the electric motor with a screen filter totally caked in a heavy, greasy film. Problem one, easily solved, was the filter. Without air circulation, the motor would overheat. Cleaning the filter took but a few minutes with some solvent and a scrubbing with an old toothbrush. But that didn't fix the buttons, and they were not accessible, mounted as they were in the underside of the case. It was evident that further dissection would be required.

A thin metal plate labelled with the function of each switch was glued over the switches. Removing it revealed the fastening screws for the switch mechanism. Five minutes later, the switches were lying on the bench and the problem was evident. Over the years, although the facing had been carefully cleaned after each usage so that the buttons were a pristine ivory colour, food particles had worked their way underneath the buttons and coated the metal shaft, building up a black residue that clogged the return springs inside and eventually prevented the shafts from pressing in.

Carefully, using Q-Tips dipped in a light solvent designed for electrical components, I cleaned each switch and shaft, then re-assembled the entire device, plugged it in, and switched it on. Success!

The blender now functions perfectly, but a cursory examination reveals that it has been opened. It hadn't been possible to remove the switch cover plate without it bending, and after it was re-glued it no longer lay completely flat. There are now small wrinkles on the faceplate that cannot be hidden.

So what?

Application

This is just like a lot of us. We spend years working at our jobs, in the church, singing in the choir, or whatever. Perhaps you're in paid Christian service (I try to avoid the term "full-time Christian service," because we are all full-time citizens of the Kingdom). Then one day it happens: you just can't get out of bed. Breakfast tastes completely flat and everything just plain gets on your nerves. In appearance you look perfectly normal, but inside is a cauldron of accumulated problems clogging the works.

With our blender, the fall to the floor had absolutely no bearing on the problem. Nothing was broken by the fall. So it is with us. Sometimes God has to knock us to the floor to attract our attention to problems building up within. We all know the story of Jonah and the storm, but take a look at Jonah's conversation with God from the belly of the fish:

Then Jonah prayed to the Lord his God from the fish's belly. And he said: "I cried out to the Lord because of my affliction, and He answered me. Out of the belly of Sheol I cried, and You heard my voice. For You cast me into the deep, into the heart of the seas, and the floods surrounded me; all Your billows and Your waves passed over me. Then I said, 'I have been cast out of Your sight; yet I will look again toward Your holy temple.' The waters surrounded me, even to my soul; the deep closed around me; weeds were wrapped around my head. I went down to the moorings of the mountains; the earth with its bars closed behind me forever; yet You have brought up my life from the pit, O Lord, my God. When my soul fainted within me, I remembered the Lord; and my prayer went up to You, into Your holy temple."

—Jonah 2:1–7

In Jonah 2:2, we hear Jonah crying out to God. He states that he was in Sheol (in Hebrew, "the all-demanding world"; in Greek, "Hades, the unknown region"), the invisible world of departed souls. This was before he was thrown into the water. He had been separated from God through running away and was literally in a hell of his own creation. God had to knock Jonah to the floor in order to get his attention. The storm and subsequently being thrown overboard *alerted* Jonah to his situation. As he sank to the bottom, he remembered the Lord and cried out (Jonah 2:7).

But let's get back to the blender. The blender is an old model held together by screws. Consequently, it can be disassembled. New blenders are made entirely of moulded plastic parts that snap together. It isn't possible to access the workings without breaking the case. Think about it! It's important for us to remain accessible to God's repair kit.

In your minds, contrast Pharaoh and Nebuchadnezzar. When God initially tried to deal with Pharaoh, Pharaoh, hardened his heart against God, but when God disciplined Nebuchadnezzar, Nebuchadnezzar accepted the chastisement and worshipped God, for his heart remained soft and open to the moving of the Spirit. In the parable of the Samaritan, two church leaders passed the wounded businessman on the highway before the Samaritan came along. Both men of God saw the stranger's plight and had the ability to provide succour, yet neither saw an opportunity to serve God and show compassion. Neither heard, understood, or responded to the voice of the Spirit. Their religious armour left no access plate to the workings of their hearts.

Which brings us to the clogged screen. Since I knew from the beginning that the problem was with the switch, the blender could have been made operational without needing to clean the screen. Sandy would have had a working blender, but only until the motor overheated and burnt out.

Preventive maintenance! We do it with our cars and our homes, so why should it surprise us when God recommends preventive maintenance for our souls? In fact, He initiated the concept. God gives us numerous commands to stop and smell the roses: *"Six days shalt thou labour, and do all thy work..."* (Exodus 20:9, KJV). Others? How about Matthew 5:25?

> *Agree with your adversary quickly, while you are on the way with him, lest your adversary deliver you to the judge, the judge hand you over to the officer, and you be thrown into prison.*

Or maybe Matthew 6:34:

> *Therefore do not worry about tomorrow, for tomorrow will worry about its own things. Sufficient for the day is its own trouble.*

In fact, the Sermon on the Mount is chock-full of preventive maintenance items. But preventive maintenance requires time and effort. It necessitates removing the cover plate to our conscience, habits, and inner thoughts, examining each part and then taking a prayer soaked in spiritual solvent to each clogged filter. We are constantly in contact with situations that entice us into being less than our best. Each contact, regardless of the manner in which we deal with it, results in a little bit of dirt being deposited.

When we examined the Lord's Prayer, we took a good look at the meaning behind "Forgive us our trespasses." Well, the stuff that clogs our minds, the stuff God needs to clean during preventive maintenance, are just that—trespasses.

Finally, we come to the problem that caused the blender to quit working in the first place. As was mentioned previously, the blender appeared clean and whole. But inside, the switches were stiff with congealed grease. Christ Himself had something to say about this, so I'll use His words and leave it at that:

> *Woe to you, scribes and Pharisees, hypocrites! For you cleanse the outside of the cup and dish, but inside they are full of extortion and self-indulgence. Blind Pharisee, first cleanse the inside of the cup and dish, that the outside of them may be clean also.*
>
> —Matthew 23:25–26

One final observation: all the clean-up actions are things we do ourselves. In fact, they are all commands of Christ to us. We are responsible for our inner condition. Now Christ will knock us off the table—

> *And you have forgotten the exhortation which speaks to you as to sons: "My son, do not despise the chastening of the Lord, nor be discouraged when you are rebuked by Him; for whom the Lord loves He chastens, and scourges every son whom He receives." If you endure chastening, God deals with you as with sons; for what son is there whom a father does not chasten? But if you are without chastening, of which all have become partakers, then you are illegitimate and not sons.*
>
> —Hebrews 12:5–8

—but it's then up to us to unbolt the cover plates and start the process of cleansing. I'll leave it to you to read your own ideas into the wrinkled cover plate, just to give you something to think about!

Chapter 41

Are We Christians, Sinners?

DEAR PASTOR,

I was watching one of those talk shows on television last night. The moderator, from one of those big southern Baptist churches in Memphis, I think, was going on about how we as Christians should be more empathetic with folks around us. I agree, but his reasoning caused me problems. Now, maybe he was only trying to be folksy and keep his answers a little light. If that's the case, then okay, but nevertheless it caused me a bit of grief.

So I called my brother-in-law (the Pentecostal one) and talked it over with him, and he said the same thing as the preacher. So I figured I must be wrong. But before I change my mind, my wife suggested I talk it over with you. Hence this letter.

The reason the fellow gave was that we are the same as non-Christians. We are only *sinners saved by grace*. Is this true?

So, Pastor, am I thinking a little funny, or should I try to change?

Sincerely yours,

Third Pew Back, Left-Hand Side

Dear Third Pew,

This is one of those occasions when both sides are right (in a way), but I would place your thoughts a little further to the right side than those of the moderator and your in-law. The statement you are quoting is commonly used to describe Christians, yet it seems to me that it doesn't properly convey the miracle of salvation. Bear with me for a bit and I'll try and explain what I mean.

First of all, the verb tense is wrong. It should be in the past tense. "I *was* only a sinner..." But what is a sinner? A sinner is very simply defined by Webster's as "one who sins." A sin is an action contrary to the law of God. In that sense, I suppose we are still sinners. But Webster's goes on to define sin as "a state to be condemned in the light of God's law," and that portion of the definition no longer applies.

> *There is therefore now no condemnation to those who are in Christ Jesus, who do not walk according to the flesh, but according to the Spirit. For the law of the Spirit of life in Christ Jesus has made me free from the law of sin and death.*
>
> —Romans 8:1–2

Paul goes on to explain further:

> *Who shall bring a charge against God's elect? It is God who justifies. Who is he who condemns? It is Christ who died, and furthermore is also risen, who is even at the right hand of God, who also makes intercession for us.*
>
> —Romans 8:33–34

Here we find Paul explaining that only Christ has the authority to condemn, for only He lived a life that made judgement possible. Christ demonstrated this in His dealings with the woman in John 8. Remember the story? Everyone was ready to stone the woman until Jesus intervened and gave the rules for judgement: "He who is without sin may throw the first stone." He was the only person present with the moral authority to actually pass judgement, and He refused to do so. Instead He instructed her to refrain from her immoral behaviour.

What happens when an individual requests forgiveness of God? The Pharisee asked Jesus that very question. "You must be born again," Jesus replied. You are remanufactured at the time of salvation. We still want to sin, but we are no longer sinners. It's no longer our basic nature. It is an amazing transformation that occurs. Just think of all the verses that refer to being made over:

...old things have passed away; behold, all things have become new.
—2 Corinthians 5:17

...not by works of righteousness which we have done, but according to His mercy He saved us, through the washing of regeneration and renewing of the Holy Spirit...
—Titus 3:5

And do not be conformed to this world, but be transformed by the renewing of your mind, that you may prove what is that good and acceptable and perfect will of God.
—Romans 12:2

The word "renew" doesn't mean a makeover: it means that we are reconstructed from the ground up.

Let's get back to the topic at hand. God has remade you. The core of your existence, your spirit, is now God's house. It is His holy of holies, Teflon-coated and impervious to sin. You are a citizen of Heaven and a member of the family of God. You have the right to call Him Father. Before this time, your spirit was controlled by Satan, but now he can't obtain entrance.

So are you still a sinner? Absolutely not! You are no longer condemned by your actions. Do you still sin? Absolutely, and you will spend the rest of your life trying to improve your behaviour to prove yourself worthy of the sacrifice Christ made on your behalf. Remember the verse from Paul regarding your body? ("Don't you know that your body is God's temple?") If you put Christ's cleansing of the temple into that context, you can see what I'm driving at.

In summary then, you *were* a sinner. When you confessed that Christ was Lord, He took over and remade your spirit as suitable living quarters for the Spirit. Every time you sin, you muddy up the outer temple, but the Holy of Holies remains God's dwelling place

As you grow in the Spirit, the garbage that surrounds you (mentally and morally speaking) will become more and more of an aggravation, and you will be anxious to clean it up—not so much from a feeling of guilt, although that is certainly valid, but from a feeling of shame.

So, Third Pew, does that help? I'll look for you on Sunday in your normal place, third pew back, left-hand side.

Have a great week and God bless. Pastor.

Something to think about!

Chapter 42

Trusting or Gullible?

GULLIBILITY IS ONE OF THE MOST COMMON CHARACTER TRAITS ASSIGNED TO those of us who believe Scripture is without error and that God created the earth in seven literal days. I have also seen myself described as a flat-earther, a Neanderthal, and an ignoramus, but for the sake of today's thoughts, "gullible" is sufficient. So am I? Gullible, I mean.

To answer that question, I went back to my Webster's. After reading the definitions, I have come to the conclusion that it is my detractors who are gullible. I am trusting.

> *The Lord is on my side; I will not fear. What can man do to me? The Lord is for me among those who help me; therefore I shall see my desire on those who hate me. It is better to trust in the Lord than to put confidence in man. It is better to trust in the Lord than to put confidence in princes.*
>
> —Psalms 118:6–9

If there's another word in the English language that has been abused more than "trust," I don't know what it would be. It shows up frequently in Scripture and in our songs. It's sad, though, that when many people think about trust, they consider the word "gullible" as being a near-synonym, particularly when the word is used in reference to the Christian faith. When you examine the definition, however, it's evident that nothing could be further from the truth.

Here's the definition of "trust" as extracted from my old Webster's:

1. Confidence in a person or thing because of the qualities one perceives or seems to perceive in him or it.

2. Acceptance of something as true or reliable without being able to verify it, on trust.

3. A responsibility, charge or duty involving the confidence of others.

4. The responsibility resulting from having others' confidence placed in one.

5. The person in whom or the thing in which one has confidence.

The second definition is the one most often associated with faith.

To define something is to state the precise meaning and identify the precise characteristics of something. It's easy to make the comparison between gullibility and trust if that's the only definition considered. That second definition, however, doesn't define "trust"; the first, second, third, fourth, and fifth define it collectively. If we leave out any of these phrases, we are leaving out an essential characteristic of what trust means.

As can be seen from the definition, trust is based upon evidence. We trust someone or something because of the qualities we perceive within him (the first definition). Were the three gentlemen who uttered the following statement gullible, or did they have empirical evidence to support their claim? *"Our God whom we serve is able to deliver us from the burning fiery furnace, and He will deliver us from your hand"* (Daniel 3:17). If you recall the story, they had already proven God's faithfulness in His support for their kosher dietary request. They were healthy, wealthy, and respected rulers in the land where they had once been captives.

The testimony of Scripture is here:

As for these four young men, God gave them knowledge and skill in all literature and wisdom; and Daniel had understanding in all visions and dreams. Now at the end of the days, when the king had said that they should be brought in, the chief of the eunuchs brought them in before Nebuchadnezzar. Then the king interviewed them, and among them all none was found like Daniel, Hananiah, Mishael, and Azariah; therefore they served before the king. And in all matters of wisdom and understanding about which the king examined them, he found them ten times better than all the magicians and astrologers who were in all his realm.

—Daniel 1:17–20

So these men had previous experience that had proven to them that their God was reliable.

I thought it good to declare the signs and wonders that the Most High God has worked for me. How great are His signs, and how mighty His wonders! His kingdom is an everlasting kingdom, and His dominion is from generation to generation.

—Daniel 4:2–3

Who spoke these words? Nebuchadnezzar did. Old Neb had experienced God in a way that left him no doubt as to who God was.

He did not waver at the promise of God through unbelief, but was strengthened in faith, giving glory to God, and being fully convinced that what He had promised He was also able to perform.

—Romans 4:20–21

And God is able to make all grace abound toward you, that you, always having all sufficiency in all things, may have an abundance for every good work.

—2 Corinthians 9:8

The attributes of God listed in the above scriptures have all been proven over and over again. Each of us can testify from our own lives regarding events where God has proven His faithfulness. Now pick up today's newspaper and try to find an article involving a politician, judge, scientist, doctor, or teacher that would give you a reason to "trust" what they have to say or live as they live.

The second definition stems from the first. God doesn't expect us to accept Him blindly. He has provided countless thousands of ways in which we can prove Him to be trustworthy. When a small child obeys when his father commands, "Jump and I will catch you," he does so with the assurance that Dad will indeed catch him; Dad has always done what he says he will do. Jesus said as much in one of the parables regarding sheep: "They follow me because they know my voice." In other words, "They know me and they trust me."

So, you see, trust is based upon prior knowledge.

The remaining statements in our definition describe the object or person to whom or at which the trust is directed. Before we trust something, we generally check it out first. One of the greatest compliments a person can be given is to say of them: "Their word is their bond" or "Their handshake is as good as a signed contract." This type of reputation is hard-earned, and justifiably so. God asks us to trust Him, but He also suggests that we try Him and prove Him to be worthy of that trust at the same time. His word is His bond. He will deliver what He promises, and that brings us to the second part of the definition for trust. Trust is also a verb:

1. To have faith or trust in.

2. To rely on [someone] to do something or permit [some one] to use something in the proper way.

3. To believe.

4. To entrust.

All of these aspects of trust are built upon the foundational aspects outlined in the noun. We can trust God because He has proven Himself worthy of that trust. God says that His word is true, so if one aspect of His Word is proven false, then God Himself is false. Therefore, when science makes a statement that is contrary to Scripture, it's time to check out the science *and* Scripture. God wants you to. He doesn't want you to be gullible.

Test all things; hold fast what is good.

—1 Thessalonians 5:21

Here's Psalm 34: 8, in my own words: "Check me out, and then trust me." Now here it is as written by the Psalmist:

Oh, taste and see that the Lord is good; blessed is the man who trusts in Him!

—Psalm 34:8

The definition for gullible is short and succinct: "easily deceived or cheated."

The daily news is filled with stories of politicians, teachers, businessmen, and even scientists who have been compromised, caught in lies, cheated, or have literally stolen millions from people who trusted them. These are the same people who deny creation, extol Darwin, ridicule our faith, and call us fools for believing that God could even exist, let alone be responsible for the formation of this earth. "I lied about this or that," they say, "but you can believe me when I say there is no God or that evolution is fact. The evidence is overwhelming; the science is settled."

Compare the above definitions of trust and gullible. On the one hand, we have God who has proven Himself as trustworthy, and on the other hand we have those groups mentioned above. Now answer this question: are you trusting or gullible?

Something to think about!

Chapter 43

Materials at Hand

It happened on the same night that the Lord said to him, "Arise, go down against the camp, for I have delivered it into your hand. But if you are afraid to go down, go down to the camp with Purah your servant, and you shall hear what they say; and afterward your hands shall be strengthened to go down against the camp." Then he went down with Purah his servant to the outpost of the armed men who were in the camp.

—Judges 7:9–11

YOU HAVE TO FEEL FOR GIDEON. IN ANSWER TO GOD'S CALL TO PURGE THE land of the Midianites, he sent out a call for troops. The people responded by the tens of thousands and Gideon was suddenly the leading general of a respectably sized army. Within a few days, however, God had whittled the army down to just a few hundred souls. "Gideon, you have to trust me," He said.

Like all good leaders, Gideon next went out to spy out the opposing forces. There was no point in counting them, because there were just too many:

Now the Midianites and Amalekites, all the people of the East, were lying in the valley as numerous as locusts; and their camels were without number, as the sand by the seashore in multitude.

—Judges 7:12

Gideon was able to spy out their defensive positions, however, and listen in on the fears and rumours going about the camp. Just imagine now the conversation between God and Gideon:

Gideon: Okay, Father, it's easy to see that they are demoralized and we should be able to succeed in terrorizing their camp, particularly if we can get all those animals to stampede. If you could please start an earthquake or landslide, or maybe cause a flash flood to come down the wadi at the right time, we should be able to drive them back down the valley without destroying ourselves in the process.

The Lord: Nice idea, but instead, get each man to light a lamp inside their water jug and then surround the place. Oh, and don't forget to bring your trumpets.

And then there was Noah: the original do-it-yourself type. God commanded him to build an ark. Before he could do that, though, he would have had to cut the trees, split them into planks, drill them out to enable them to be pegged to the frame, shape them, and so on and so on. It took him over a hundred years! I suspect that along about year ten or so, there were some fascinating conversations between him and God.

Noah: This is a big job, Lord. So far I only have enough wood cut to do about half of the frame. At this rate, it's going to take me about a hundred years.

The Lord: Yup.

Noah: You are going to flood out this place, right?

The Lord: Yup.

Noah: I can't do this, Lord. It's just too big a task to achieve on my own. I need your divine intervention to finish this thing. Wouldn't it be possible for you to maybe help a little?

The Lord: I already did. You have three sons, don't you?

Take a moment and read the parable regarding the talents:

For the kingdom of heaven is like a man traveling to a far country, who called his own servants and delivered his goods to them. And to one he gave five talents, to another two, and to another one, to each according to his own ability; and immediately he went on a journey.
—Matthew 25:14–15

Notice that the master didn't divide the talents equally amongst them. Also notice that the guy who didn't do anything was the one to whom he entrusted the least. Could it be that the master had been observing the work habits of his employees for some time before his departure and already had a fair idea of what each person could be entrusted to achieve?

Each story is the same. God supplied Gideon with just enough to accomplish the task, provided that Gideon would trust God. There was to be no human accepting the credit. The plan of attack was God's, the victory was to be the Lord's, and the tools to be used were common everyday objects. But they were sufficient. God gave Noah a job to do, and then He gave him the health and labour force he needed to complete the ark.

In the parable of the talents, one thing is often overlooked. The three servants were left on their own. They received no instructions as to what the master wanted them to do—and they received no reward or recognition *until the master returned*. Only then did they hear these words: *"Well done, good and faithful servant: you have been faithful over a few things, I will make you ruler over many things"* (Matthew 25:23). We are often led to believe that if we're faithful in a few things, God will reward us. We keep looking for those greater benefits. Well, I hate to be the bearer of bad news, but guess what? Those benefits may not materialise before your summons to the throne room of Heaven.

Here's a list of hypothetical questions you may hear on judgement day.

Eight Things that Won't Matter When the Books Are Opened

1. The age and model of your car won't matter. What will matter is the number of people you drove who needed transportation.

2. The size of your house won't matter. What will matter is the number of people whom you made welcome as guests.

3. Your neighbourhood won't matter. What will matter is how you treated your neighbours.

4. The designer labels on your clothes won't matter. What will matter is the number of people whom you helped clothe.

5. The size of your paycheck won't matter. What will matter is the moral compromises you made to earn it.

6. Your position and job title won't matter. What will matter is whether you gave your employer a 100% effort.

7. The number of names on the list of people you knew won't matter. What will matter is the names on the list of people whom you befriended.

8. The number of promotions you received won't matter. What will matter is the effort you made to promote others.

Your responses may give you something to think about.

Chapter 44

Loving God

Then one of them, a lawyer, asked Him a question, testing Him, and saying, "Teacher, which is the great commandment in the law?"

Jesus said to him, "'You shall love the Lord your God with all your heart, with all your soul, and with all your mind.' This is the first and great commandment."

—Matthew 22:35–38

WITH THE EXCEPTION OF JOHN 3:16, I DOUBT IF THERE'S ANOTHER VERSE IN all of Scripture that is as well-known as Matthew 22:37. I suspect we can all rattle it off with scarcely a thought, and most times I do just that. It's an easy verse to be happy with. And then comes the reply: "Love God with all your heart, soul, and mind." I can do that. The Pharisees threw this question out at Jesus in an effort to trap Him, so there must be more to it than appears at first, but what?

The first part requires me to love God with my heart. What could be simpler? God is good and is responsible for all good things I encounter upon this earth. He made the trees and flowers and He provided me with my friends and my wife and family. He has given me the promise of eternal life, so what is there not to love? So yes, I will love God with my heart.

I missed a word in that last sentence. The word is "all," and that's what triggered these thoughts. According to my old friend Webster, as an adjective "all" means "the whole quantity of," whilst as a noun the meaning becomes "everything, one's total possessions." If I literally apply these definitions to Matthew 22:37, the end result should be that

I have no love left for my wife, family, friends, or indeed anyone or anything else left on the planet.

Whoops!

"Now, wait a minute, Lord. You don't really mean that, do you?" But that's what it says, and that's where our obedience normally ends, right at the start of the process of obeying the most important commandment. We don't even get past the first sentence. When it comes to the love of our hearts, we tend to put our wives and husbands, children and parents at least on par with God. But see what Jesus had to say about this very issue:

> Then He said to another, "Follow Me."
>
> But he said, "Lord, let me first go and bury my father."
>
> Jesus said to him, "Let the dead bury their own dead, but you go and preach the kingdom of God."
>
> And another also said, "Lord, I will follow You, but let me first go and bid them farewell who are at my house."
>
> But Jesus said to him, "No one, having put his hand to the plow, and looking back, is fit for the kingdom of God."
>
> —Luke 9:59–62

This is not an easy thing to think about, because it means changing absolutely every one of my priorities. It means I must totally void myself of all my love for the people around me, and that is where human nature catches us every time. We hold a little back or, to put it even more bluntly, Satan lets out a great big, "Gotcha!"

We have it all wrong. Christ tells us to love our neighbour in the verses that follow in Matthew, and that would seem to be a contradiction. After all, if we have expended all our love upon Christ, what is left? The apostle John has the answer:

> Beloved, let us love one another, for love is of God; and everyone who loves is born of God and knows God. 8 He who does not love does not know God, for God is love.

Even the best love I can give Christ is flawed. It has been con-
taminated by ten thousand years of increasing separation from God.
My outlook is coloured by the things I see and read and hear that are
displeasing to God but are simply part of the twenty-first century;
billboards, signs, newspapers, books, and conversation on the tram all
reflect a human race that has long abandoned any pretence of religion.
And that doesn't even begin to touch on my own character flaws. So
my love is like my righteousness:

> But we are all like an unclean thing, and all our righteousnesses are
> like filthy rags; we all fade as a leaf, and our iniquities, like the wind,
> have taken us away.
>
> —Isaiah 64:6

When you think about it, God really isn't getting much of a bargain. What does He give in return?

> ...that Christ may dwell in your hearts through faith; that you, being
> rooted and grounded in love, may be able to comprehend with all the
> saints what is the width and length and depth and height—to know
> the love of Christ which passes knowledge; that you may be filled with
> all the fullness of God. Now to Him who is able to do exceedingly
> abundantly above all that we ask or think, according to the power
> that works in us, to Him be glory in the church by Christ Jesus to all
> generations, forever and ever. Amen.
>
> —Ephesians 3:17–21

> And my God shall supply all your need according to His riches in glory
> by Christ Jesus.
>
> —Philippians 4:19

> Blessed be the God and Father of our Lord Jesus Christ, who has bless-
> ed us with every spiritual blessing in the heavenly places in Christ...
>
> —Ephesians 1:3

Seems to me we're getting the best of the deal. And lest you think that Scripture is referring only to feel-better philosophical stuff, think back to the first man. God saw that Adam needed someone to share his earth with. Adam needed love and friendship and all the rest of the good things about relationships, and He supplied it in spades.

> *Then the rib which the Lord God had taken from man He made into a woman, and He brought her to the man. And Adam said: "This is now bone of my bones And flesh of my flesh; She shall be called Woman, Because she was taken out of Man." Therefore a man shall leave his father and mother and be joined to his wife, and they shall become one flesh. And they were both naked, the man and his wife, and were not ashamed.*
>
> —Genesis 2:22–25

If I read my Bible correctly, I am commanded to love God with all my heart. When I do that, I have none of my old-nature love left for my family or friends, so God fills my heart with His eternal everlasting love!

Good deal! Now that's something to think about!

Chapter 45

Can You Come Up with Another Explanation?

THE SURVIVAL OF THE FITTEST! THIS IS THE EXPRESSION DARWIN COINED TO define the concept of evolution. It was based upon the premise that constant changes can be observed within the animal kingdom. If a particular trait enables a particular animal to outwit, outfight, or outsurvive a similar creature that doesn't have that trait, then the former will become dominant and the latter extinct.

It sort of makes sense, until you take a closer look—and then the whole concept becomes nonsensical, at least in my mind. As I explain, you can decide whether or not to agree.

I love watching hummingbirds. Most varieties are found only in the Americas, so for my European friends, a hummingbird is about the size of my thumb. Their wings flap at least twice as fast as most birds you may be familiar with. This rapid wing movement is responsible for producing the characteristic humming sound that's the source of the bird's name. They have a bill that's quite long, almost the same length as its body, and tubular shaped.

The hummingbird is capable of stopping in mid-flight, hovering, flying sideways, and even flying backwards, just like a helicopter does. These flight characteristics are unique to the hummingbird. Hummingbirds drink nectar, a sweet liquid inside certain flowers. Like bees, they're able to assess the amount of sugar in the nectar they eat; they reject flower types that produce nectar that is less than ten percent sugar and prefer those whose sugar content is higher. Nectar is a poor source of nutrients, so hummingbirds meet their needs for protein, amino acids, vitamins, and minerals by preying on insects and spiders.

In order to hover and insert its bill into a blossom the wings of a hummingbird cycle at up to one hundred times per second to enable the bird to hold position.

Let us list the unique (or at least rarely duplicated) characteristics of the hummingbird:

- They fly backwards, and hover.
- They feed on nectar.
- They have a tubular bill uniquely suitable for reaching into flowers.
- They are very small.
- They have a high pulse rate.
- They have a high rate of metabolism.
- They are able to go dormant at night when food sources aren't readily available.

The first problem confronting an evolutionist, of course, would be identifying the hummingbird's ancestors—that is, another bird or a fossilized one with which the hummingbird shares at least some of its unique characteristics. The next step is finding the pivotal change. What characteristic gave the hummingbird a leg (or wing) up on its ancestor and contributed to its successful evolution? Unfortunately, with the exception of its bill and size, identifying the unique features of this little guy require a live specimen. But maybe we can develop a plausible scenario for why the hummingbird family came to differentiate itself from its common ancestors.

Assume either a dearth of small insects or the existence of fierce competition for the available insect supply in the avian community. One particular morning, a small bird comes to rest upon the stem of a plant that has just blossomed. The poor little fellow is tired. Every time he locates a flight of mosquitoes, a flock of barn swallows chases him away. He's hungry and frustrated and terrified about what his spouse will say when he returns to the nest with no food for the kids. As he sits there brooding, a wonderful odour wafts across his beak. He identifies the odour with the blossom under which he is resting. He plunges his beak and head into the blossom and scrapes some of the tiny drops of liquid that he finds there into his mouth. Delicious! His problem is solved.

Quickly, he fills his bill with the juicy sweet nectar and dashes home. Fortunately, the little tyke's spouse shares his taste in food. She praises his ingenuity, he shows her the blossoms, they teach the kids, and the development of a whole new species has begun. Over the next several centuries, successive generations developed longer bills to enable them to more readily feed upon the blossoms. They developed the ability to hover and fly backwards and the other traits that make them hummingbirds.

Nice story, isn't it? And that's all it is—a story. For a hummingbird to be a hummingbird requires all of the traits identified above. When you remove one, the hummingbird as a species ceases to exist. No bird exists that has thirty percent of a hummingbird's characteristics, because with the possible exception of its manoeuvrability, none of its assets are assets at all unless they all exist together.

Consider the long bill. True, it serves some purpose as a spear to execute a particularly juicy arachnid morsel for lunch, but other insect-catching birds manage just fine with proportionately small bills. Without the ability to hover, a hummingbird would be unable to feed on nectar. It's the only approach whereby it can insert its proboscis into a flower blossom. Without a long bill, a hummingbird would be unable to reach the nectar in the blossoms. Without the ability to fly backwards, a hummingbird would be unable to extract its bill from the blossom after feeding without tumbling to the ground. If it were any larger, it would be compelled to spend the vast majority of its life just eating in order to sustain the metabolism needed to sustain its mode of flight. As it is, they consume several times their own weight in nectar daily. So only a small bird would have been a candidate for the modifications needed to become a hummingbird.

The rapid wing motion required to hover requires a far greater pulse rate than your average avian specimen. The high pulse rate requires the body to provide food in a hurry, hence the high metabolism. But when not actually flying, the hummingbird has the ability to go partially dormant, thus conserving energy and reducing the metabolic rate until it's actually needed. It all goes together. There is no intermediate step. And God looked at the hummingbird and said, "It is good."

Choose your own favourite bird or animal. Each has characteristics that make it unique. As for the hummingbird, did it develop those characteristics to take advantage of a dwindling food supply, as my simple story suggests? Or did a great and creative God create a tiny creature with the ability to dine on flowers, like a bee, just because it pleased Him to do so and because the end result would be so breathtakingly beautiful and graceful?

There are only the two choices.

There is none so blind as he who will not see![16]

Something to think about!

---

16 Attributed to John Heywood, 1546.

Chapter 46

Who Sinned?

Rabbi, who sinned, this man or his parents, that he was born blind?
—John 9:2

As you may recall, the disciples who asked Jesus this question had previously assumed that the blind man's misfortunes were a direct result of past sins, either his own or those of his forbearers. Jesus' answer, of course, was that neither of them had sinned.

After the financial crash of 2008, the banks were in a mess. Many individuals watched their savings dwindle or disappear as investments were ravaged by reality. Christians and non-Christians alike went from prosperity to poverty overnight (at least in their minds). It was an all-inclusive financial bloodbath.

The mantra of several outspoken evangelists has been: "You have not because you ask not." They have also equated poverty with a lack of faith. Some churches associated the recent financial meltdown as God's punishment for greed, or they gleefully rubbed their hands together and sneered at those proponents of the prosperity gospel who had seen their achievements vanish in a matter of weeks. So does the fact that many believers lost money mean that they sinned or demonstrated a lack of faith? Are the events of 2008 a repudiation of the entire prosperity gospel?

Good questions. But I'm not even going to try and answer them, because I don't believe the replies are significant. The answers would be either focussed on trying to defend previous decisions or sound like I'm saying "I told you so," and neither is particularly beneficial. Instead I will leave it to you to formulate your own arguments.

I have learnt, or been reminded of, several of Jesus' basic teachings as a result of the financial crisis. The first is taken from Matthew 6:

> *Therefore do not worry, saying, "What shall we eat?" or "What shall we drink?" or "What shall we wear?" For after all these things the Gentiles seek. For your heavenly Father knows that you need all these things. But seek first the kingdom of God and His righteousness, and all these things shall be added to you. Therefore do not worry about tomorrow, for tomorrow will worry about its own things. Sufficient for the day is its own trouble.*
>
> —Matthew 6:31–34

Very simply, we need to continue to focus upon completing the tasks God has set out for us.

Now, it's hard to achieve this when we spend valuable hours watching the markets rise and fall. Can we actually influence the outcome by doing so? Many are justifiably concerned about the security of their present positions, but is worrying about the loss going to increase the possibility that our jobs will remain secure? If we are doing the work God wants us to be doing, He will provide. That is the promise in Matthew 6: 33, but it may not be our current positions. What He wants us to do is focus on the work alone. Supply and Services is His department. The danger in the current economic crisis is that we will ignore His work and indulge in fruitless attempts to influence issues over which we have no control.

The second teaching I was reminded of is also found in the Sermon, but it comes at the tail end of Matthew 7. Here, Jesus details the differences between a citizen of Heaven and a citizen of earth. On a normal day, He says, you cannot tell the difference. Both houses have four walls, shutters, and a solid door. The dog plays outside in both backyards and the washing hangs on the line. When trouble strikes (the storm), the foundations of the home belonging to the earthly citizen are dissolved by the flood and the house crumbles into the torrent, taking its occupants to certain death. The home of the citizen of

Heaven is constructed upon a foundation of bedrock. When trouble strikes, the foundation remains solid and the house endures, protecting its occupants until the flood subsides.

Our current financial crisis is global. It's also indiscriminate. It doesn't care what denomination you belong to or whether you are Christian or atheist. Scripture records that *nothing* happens that is exceptional to us in particular, so this financial crisis is just part of living. Anxiety causes health problems. Worrying over money contributes to family arguments and marriage breakdowns. How Christians deal with a very real problem may well influence the non-believer who has been watching, trying to determine whether Christianity is worth the investment.

I suspect many believers had built their future upon Freddie or the Lehman Brothers, so the foundations of their financial security crumbled. But if the foundations for their lives rest upon the truths to which Matthew referred, they will survive. The manner in which we will come out the other end depends entirely upon whether our foundation (or god) was our money or whether it was ultimately Jesus Christ.

Something to think about!

Chapter 47

Keeping the Temple Clean

I HEARD A COUPLE OF MINISTERS TALKING. THEY WERE DISCUSSING WHAT portion of the service they found most difficult. Amongst the answers, the most common seemed to be baby dedications. They never knew what to expect. One child would lie sleeping through the whole process whilst another would scream his/her heart out, and a third might choose the moment when the minister was holding her to regurgitate half of her last meal. Many pastors have now adopted the process of allowing parents to continue holding their infants, avoiding the difficulties of having to comfort a distressed child or keeping the more inquisitive from pulling on his glasses or removing his microphone.

I have seen some adults who are never seen without an entourage of children. You've probably met them yourselves. They have balloons in their pockets and are always pulling quarters out from behind the ears of their young fans. When they start to tell a story, the noisiest of children becomes hushed and waits in eager anticipation. When a child in their care falls and skins a knee or breaks out in tears, their arms are open to comfort them. These people listen attentively to every word the little ones speak, and the children wait patiently for the end of the story before saying anything. In a word, children trust them and love them. Children recognize these grown-ups instinctively. They don't need to be told that this or that adult can be trusted or is a good person; they just know.

When Jesus entered the temple on the day He entered Jerusalem as Messiah, the first thing He did was get rid of the moneychangers and those who were selling animals and birds for sacrifice. If you want some idea of what it must have been like, go down to the local farmer's market or to an auction sale. The sounds are the same. Apart from the noise of frightened animals expressing their displeasure at being in such an unnatural place, there would have been pitchmen attracting attention, explaining why theirs were the best animals to buy. There would have been bargain hunters seeking the best prices and others arguing that they had been cheated.

What about the smells? An animal emits some objectionable odours, and yes, bodily effluent when frightened. And there would have been garbage, lots of it. There always is. It's an integral part of any market: people shouting out prices and bargains whilst bargain hunters jostle the unwary for a more advantageous position, causing bits of lunch, drinks, and containers to be dropped and abandoned. By the end of the day, the square is an absolute mess, but with the merchants gone it becomes strangely subdued and silent.

So too it must have been in the outer temple once Jesus had finished the cleansing process. The normal noises of commerce were gone, but instead of silence the church leaders heard the cries of children as they ran and skipped and clapped and shouted to each other in jubilation. I suspect the children had never before had the square to themselves, an open space available for games and song. Probably they had never before heard their own voices echo off the marble walls of this imposing building. So they sang, but to the temple rulers the song was the sound of lost business opportunities and decreased profits.

Children trusted Jesus. He was one of those adults who always had time for them. They didn't treat Him as an elder, with silent respect and obedience. Instead, when we see them they treat Him as a friend. He must have had some great stories to tell. They just loved being around Him. They knew who He was. He was the promised Son of David, but more importantly, He was their friend.

But when the chief priests and the scribes saw the wonderful things that He had done, and the children who were shouting in the temple, "Hosanna to the Son of David," they became indignant and said to Him, "Do You hear what these children are saying?" And Jesus said to them, "Yes; have you never read, 'OUT OF THE MOUTH OF

INFANTS AND NURSING BABIES YOU HAVE PREPARED PRAISE FOR YOURSELF'?"
—Matthew 21:15–16, NASB (emphasis added)

I doubt very much if the children had ever cheered on one of the priests. Like those priests, do I find the children an annoyance as they stare at me over their parents' shoulders or crawl underneath my legs in a vain attempt to escape the indignation of having to sit still? Do I rejoice when they leave for their own programme so that I can finally concentrate on the business at hand, or do I try and join with them in their games and worship as Jesus did? Are children an integral part of our worship experience?

Something to think about!

Chapter 48

The Bible Says...

IN MY STUDY, I AM SURROUNDED BY HUNDREDS OF BOOKS RANGING FROM Josephus to a number of historical biographies to dozens of novels. Through my computer, I have access to a global library exceeding tens of thousands more books. It's an impressive resource. Many of you have similar collections, or at least have access to like resources. This is the question for today: what is your final authority when you desperately need an answer?

This is no idle question. Consider these scenarios:

1. You have just finished working on a particularly difficult project for your employer, and it has evolved successfully for the firm. Instead of receiving accolades, however, you are called to your immediate supervisor's office and told that with the completion, there is no longer a need for your services.

2. You arrive home from work one evening to find the front door pried open. Your flat has been trashed. All those treasured items from your family have been smashed onto the floor, and several valuable keepsakes are missing. To top it all off, the intruders have stolen your computer, and it contained all of your account and investment information, including passwords. A quick call to the bank soon reveals that your accounts have been cleaned out.

3. You are a teacher in the local junior high school and one of the students decides that the reason his grades are so poor is because you have a personal grudge against him (you don't). In order to obtain revenge for your perceived vendetta, he initiates a smear campaign against you that accuses you of having abused him. The records appear to support him in that you had, on several occasions, ordered him to stay after class. During these periods, you attempted to aid him. Unfortunately, it's now your word against hers.

What are you going to do? Where do you turn? What is your plan for dealing with these life-shattering experiences? Each of us has our own way of responding when trouble hits. Some will hit the bottle, some will enter a state of denial, and some will seek revenge. Others will seek advice from a psychiatrist, lawyer, or minister. How many of us will first reach for the Word?

Real vs. Theoretical

On issues dealing with church and theology, most of us are satisfied that these words indicate the final authority, and we sincerely believe them. But most of us separate our religion from "real life" experiences. Why is that? Could it be that we don't really want to find a solution? Are we afraid to find God's solution? Are we just plain too advanced a civilization to believe that a book written two thousand years ago could have any practical relevance today?

Forgetting for a moment that he lived three thousand years ago, read what David had to say in Psalm 119, and compare it to the anguish or worry you have felt.

How many are the days of Your servant? When will You execute judgment on those who persecute me? The proud have dug pits for me, which is not according to Your law. All Your commandments are faithful; they persecute me wrongfully; help me! They almost made an end of me on earth, but I did not forsake Your precepts. Revive me

*according to Your lovingkindness, so that I may keep the testimony of
Your mouth. Forever, O Lord, Your word is settled in heaven. Your
faithfulness endures to all generations; You established the earth, and
it abides. They continue this day according to Your ordinances, for
all are Your servants. Unless Your law had been my delight, I would
then have perished in my affliction. I will never forget Your precepts,
for by them You have given me life. I am Yours, save me; for I have
sought Your precepts. The wicked wait for me to destroy me, but I will
consider Your testimonies.*

—Psalm 119:84–95

And you thought you had problems! Here's a guy who faced the
worst the world could throw at him. In the first few verses, he sees no
solutions at all. He's down and discouraged, and at that moment he
cries out to God. Help! Notice the little bit of self-justification. Like all
of us, he has to remind God that he's been a good boy and is therefore
worthy of help (119:87), but then he realises that it's only because of
God's goodness that he can expect any help (119:88–91).

Read 119:92 again. Paraphrased, it says, "If it wasn't for your word
O Lord I would have died."

What is it about this book that makes it so unique? First of all, it's
a series of absolutes. There's no conditional yes or no. It wasn't written
with an if-it-feels-good mentality. The Bible leaves no room for wish-
ful thinking or relativism. It states simply and precisely what is right,
what is wrong, and provides the answers. It never leaves you with a
bewildered look on your face. In other words, it provides a foundation
upon which you can confidently build your life, knowing that your
decisions are good ones.

Final Authority

What makes this book the final authority? First of all, the term "Bible"
never appears in the Bible. Whenever reference is made to these writings, two names dominate. The first name used is "Scripture."

And beginning at Moses and all the Prophets, He expounded to them
in all the Scriptures *the things concerning Himself.*
—Luke 24:27 (emphasis added)

"Scripture" shares the same root in Greek as our word *graph*. It actually means "that which is written." This is not the Koran. It's not the product of a man's dreams. Instead, Almighty God caused His thoughts to be written. He spoke directly to each writer. I get the feeling that none of the writers ever sat down one day and decided to write. Scripture gives the impression that these authors wrote in spite of themselves. They were compelled.

...knowing this first, that no prophecy of Scripture is of any private
interpretation, for prophecy never came by the will of man, *but*
holy men of God spoke as they were moved by the Holy Spirit.
—*2 Peter 1:20–21 (emphasis added)*

Scripture provides us with insight. It grafts onto paper thoughts that reflect the very mind of God.

The second name used for Scripture can be found in Jesus' prayer for His disciples:

I have given them Your word; *and the world has hated them because*
they are not of the world, just as I am not of the world. I do not pray
that You should take them out of the world, but that You should keep
them from the evil one. They are not of the world, just as I am not of the
world. Sanctify them by Your truth. Your word *is truth.*
—John 17:14–17 (emphasis added)

In the last four words, we have the reason for being able to absolutely rely on Scripture. It is true. Really, what more needs to be said?

This is the stone wall against which all of Satan's forces will shatter themselves, so he very carefully tries to avoid it. This is the same stunt he pulled on Eve. He tries to change truth from being absolute to having some degree of flexibility. Truth for contemporary people has thus become relative, yet the definition doesn't provide that degree of flexibility. Take a look. Here's what Webster's has to say about the word "true": "In agreement with fact; faithful to a cause or principle; genuine, accurate, correct, sincere."

God has never tried to deceive us regarding His intentions. His Word spells out exactly what the future holds for humanity; indeed, for all living creatures. The Japanese railway system has a well-established and well-deserved reputation for punctuality. Knowing this, it would be a very foolish man who would bet against the schedule and deliberately arrive late for his trip.

God's Word has a well-established and well-deserved reputation for accuracy. No scientist, philosopher, or historian has been able to identify a single error in fact: not ever. Many of the prophecies in Scripture have been proven to be totally fulfilled. Modern history texts provide testimony to the accuracy of the prophecies written down by Isaiah, by Jeremiah, and the rest of the Old Testament crew. Knowing this, you would think that only a very foolish man would bet against the remaining prophecies coming to pass by ignoring God's call for repentance. Yet that is what we do.

Whether we like it or not, and whether we're in agreement with what the Word says or not, doesn't matter at all in the end.

And the Lord God commanded the man, saying, "Of every tree of the garden you may freely eat; but of the tree of the knowledge of good and evil you shall not eat, for in the day that you eat of it you shall surely die." ...Then the serpent said to the woman, "You will not surely die."
—Genesis 2:16–17, 3:4

Richard Dawkins said, "Religious faith not only lacks evidence, its independence from evidence is its pride and joy, shouted from the rooftops."[17]

Pope Leo X was reported to have said, "It has served us well, this myth of Christ."

The Bible says,

---

17 Richard Dawkins, "Is Science a Religion?" *The Humanist* (January/February 1997), 26–27.

Jesus saith unto him, I am the way, the truth, and the life: no man cometh unto the Father, but by me.

—John 14:6, KJV

So who are you going to believe? Something to think about!

Chapter 49

Only One Way

DEAR PASTOR,

What a problem! A couple of weeks back, you preached on salvation and made it sound as though Christianity is the only game in town when it comes to being saved. Isn't that being more than a little bit presumptuous? My brother-in-law, not Billy from the Pentecostal Assembly but Chester, was visiting with us from Salt Lake and he said that you didn't know what you were talking about. "Lots of groups preach salvation," he says. The wife and I have been witnessing to him for months, and now he won't even talk to us. It took forever to get him to come with us to church, and then you had to floor him with that one. Were you exaggerating to make your point or do you really have some basis in fact for making such a statement? Give me something to say to help smooth things over.

Sincerely yours,

Third Pew Back Left-Hand Side

* * *

So who is correct here? Is it the pastor, with his statement that only Christianity offers salvation, or is it Third Pew's brother-in-law? Think about it!

* * *

Dear Third Pew,

If I were to avoid making controversial statements in a sermon, it wouldn't be long before I wasn't saying anything of importance at all. What I must do, though, is ensure that I can support what I say, either logically, historically, or through Scripture, with the latter being my primary authority. I feel quite confident that my argument can be substantiated. Now, whether Chester will accept my arguments is another question entirely, but we will pray that he can.

First off, let us define salvation. According to Webster's, salvation means:

> **the act of saving from destruction or catastrophe, especially the saving of the soul from sin or its consequences—the condition of being saved—something that saves.**

Salvation is not something we can accomplish on our own. It's the result of an external force redeeming a soul, and it is a uniquely spiritual word. You really have to be in dire straits before the term "salvation" can be applied to your rescue, unless of course the person reporting the event is trying to dramatize the event. It suggests the ultimate in rescue. But in all events, it is the result of second-party intervention; it is never the result of personal actions.

That leads us directly back to religions other than Christianity. For these religions, the most common view of eternal rewards provides Heaven as payment for services rendered, or as a reward for good behaviour. To give a well-known example, think about Islam's promise of multiple virgins to a man who dies fighting for his faith. For those not on the benefits' end of this golden opportunity, Islam provides a series of tasks, which if faithfully completed will also lead one to heaven.

The Hindu religion talks about the wheel of life, with each rotation bringing people the opportunity to progress higher if they succeed in pleasing the gods, until eternal life in heaven is attained and they arc finally let off the wheel.

Simply put, in all other religions, heaven is a reward. It is earned. An individual can save himself by doing good works, by dying for his faith, by giving money to the church, or through a myriad of other tasks dependent upon the faith in question.

Christianity says,

> *For by grace you have been saved through faith, and that not of your-selves; it is the gift of God, not of works, lest anyone should boast.*
> —Ephesians 2:8–9

> *For there is one God and one Mediator between God and men, the Man Christ Jesus, 6 who gave Himself a ransom for all...*
> —1 Timothy 2:5–6

If you are buying your way into Heaven, earning your way into Heaven, or winning a place in Heaven, then you aren't meeting the definition of salvation. There is no rescue or saving involved at all; it's simply an end goal attainable through following a designated route.

When you think about it, the notion of achieving Heaven in this fashion is fully in keeping with one of the very first bits of deception that Satan worked upon the human race. Listen to what he said to Eve:

> *Then the serpent said to the woman, "You will not surely die. For God knows that in the day you eat of it your eyes will be opened, and you will be like God, knowing good and evil."*
> —Genesis 3:4–5

God had told Adam not to touch the fruit, because if he did, he would die. Satan said, "You won't die. Rather, you will be just like God." God says,

> *Neither is there salvation in any other: for there is none other name under heaven given among men, whereby we must be saved.*
> —Acts 4:12, KJV

But Satan says that heaven is yours by right if you follow the directions laid out in whatever form of religion you wish to follow.

Only Christianity matches the definition of salvation. Only in Christianity do we find a route whereby we can surrender our sin-earned concept of being like God and rely on an external Truth, God Himself, to provide a guaranteed future beyond death. Christianity specifies that salvation is the result of God intervening in our lives, not a result of any good deeds or good behaviour on our part. For as Isaiah said, *"all our righteousnesses are like filthy rags"* (Isaiah 64:6).

My dear friend, I hope these few words will help you convince your brother-in-law. We will be praying for you.

Yours in Christ, Pastor.

Something to think about!

Chapter 50

Is God Our Friend?

I RECEIVED THE FOLLOWING LETTER A WHILE BACK, AND IT CAUSED ME TO pause and consider the true depths of the relationship we are supposed to enjoy with Christ. Rather than paraphrase the note, it seemed more expedient to simply reproduce the letter and start from there:

> *You say that God was a friend of Moses—is that true? Is God our friend? I have always learned that we are a friend of God, but that nowhere in the Bible does it say that God is a friend to us. He is our Creator; our Father. He loves us unconditionally but we are to be fearfully in awe of Him as God, not as a friend. Does the Bible say that God is our friend? Is there separation of us being His friend and Him not being our friend? I do get that because as much as my dad tells me that we are friends, he is still my dad and I put him above me and respect him that much more than I do my friends. God is certainly higher than any friend I could ever imagine. Do they tell us that so that we don't put God in a box and try to make Him more buddy-buddy less Deity and stop fearing Him?*

Is God our friend? He is our Creator. He is our Saviour. He is our Counsellor. These are all true statements. The last sentence of the letter identifies the problem with God being our friend, and that, I think, stems from our ideas of the nature of friendship. As usual, I consulted Webster's. A friend is

someone on terms of affection and regard for another who is neither relative nor lover. Someone who freely supports and helps out of good will. An ally, an acquaintance.

So how does your concept of God fit into that definition? Is He "an ally, an acquaintance"? Ally is a beautiful word to describe God's desired relationship with us. As a verb, the word means to unite in an alliance by treaty when the alliance refers to countries, or by marriage when the reference is to families. Scripture constantly refers to the church as being "the bride of Christ." So we have an alliance between believers and God through the marriage of the Lamb and the church. Since "ally" is synonymous with "friend," it isn't stretching things to say that the concept of friendship is inextricably woven into God's plan for us for eternity.

John 3:16 states that God loved the world so much that He sent His Son. In the meantime, we denizens of earth were merrily rejecting Him and replacing Him with Zeus, Adonis, Baal, Astarte, and myriad other lies we had labelled "god." God loved us so much that He sent His son to die. That thought certainly satisfies the first part of the definition above, doesn't it? He had so much regard for us, who were in no way related to Him, that he freely gave. Yes, I would say that God truly wants to be our friend.

Below are a number of references that all refer to God's friendship with man throughout history.

So the Lord spoke to Moses face to face, as a man speaks to his friend. And he would return to the camp, but his servant Joshua the son of Nun, a young man, did not depart from the tabernacle.
—Exodus 33:11

Then He said, "Hear now My words: If there is a prophet among you, I, the Lord, make Myself known to him in a vision; I speak to him in a dream. Not so with My servant Moses; he is faithful in all My house. I speak with him face to face, even plainly, and not in dark sayings; and he sees the form of the Lord. Why then were you not afraid to speak against My servant Moses?"

—Numbers 12:6–8

But since then there has not arisen in Israel a prophet like Moses, whom the Lord knew face to face...

—Deuteronomy 34:10

And the Scripture was fulfilled which says, "Abraham believed God, and it was accounted to him for righteousness." And he was called the friend of God.

—James 2:23

But you, Israel, are My servant, Jacob whom I have chosen, the descendants of Abraham My friend.

—Isaiah 41:8

Just as I was in the days of my prime, when the friendly counsel of God was over my tent.

—Job 29:4

Perhaps one of the underlying hindrances to us understanding and welcoming God's desire for our friendship is the often-cavalier attitude we exhibit towards our friends. Let me put that another way. We don't value friendship enough to include God in the concept.

Yet friendship is from God. It's a fundamental part of the original Adam creation, God's own image translated into flesh and blood. The ultimate in friendship is laid down in John 15:13:

Greater love hath no man than this, that a man lay down his life for his friends. (KJV)

Is that not exactly what Christ did for us? Except that He did it before we even knew Him. This was a major theme for John. In 1 John,

God takes the gift of His own life, which Jesus gave to us, and extends it to include ourselves and our attitude towards those around us.

> *By this we know love, because He laid down His life for us. And we also ought to lay down our lives for the brethren. But whoever has this world's goods, and sees his brother in need, and shuts up his heart from him, how does the love of God abide in him? My little children, let us not love in word or in tongue, but in deed and in truth.*
>
> —1 John 3:16–18

When you start thinking this way, it puts a much higher value on the meaning of friendship.

We miss out on a lot when we don't permit God to be our friend. We miss out on sharing our thoughts and plans; it's hard to discuss your dreams and aspirations with the King of the Universe, for He is too remote. We miss out on His advice and counselling; the Creator and Saviour is too busy a figure to permit a tête-à-tête.

I could go on, but I think you see the point. A personal relationship is essential to our physical and spiritual well-being, and it only comes through having Christ as our friend as well as our Creator, Saviour, King, etc.

There is a hymn from the 1960s that says it all. The writer uses the verses to describe all the amazing things God has done, but each verse ends with a plaintive "What is that to me?" The chorus, by contrast, starts softly and rises to a triumphant realization that God is far more than a creator—He is also a friend who stays right beside you. The hymn is titled "He's Everything to Me," by Ralph Carmichael. If you can, give it a listen. It will brighten your day.

Here is the definition for "friend" that we started off with:

Someone on terms of affection and regard for another who is neither relative nor lover. Someone who freely supports and helps out of good will. An ally, an acquaintance.

Do I value those whom I become acquainted with who are not my relatives? When I see those in need, do I freely support and help them just because they need support or help? If they are fellow believers, am I their ally? Are they friends simply through our marriage relationship within the church? That last point could supply our friend Third Pew with a plethora of questions all by itself, couldn't it?

Something to think about!

Chapter 51

Waiting for the Messiah

ANOTHER ONE OF THOSE CONCEPTS I ALWAYS THOUGHT WAS TRUE BIT THE dust the other day. I always thought the Bible taught that God promised the Messiah right after He threw Adam out of the garden. By that, I mean that everyone, from Adam to Malachi, was looking for Christ's coming to introduce the New Heaven and the New Earth.

But that notion doesn't stand up to close inspection at all. The quote in Genesis that's used for the basis of this (mis)understanding is:

> *And I will put enmity between you and the woman, and between your seed and her seed; He shall bruise you on the head, and you shall bruise him on the heel.*
>
> —Genesis 3:15, NASB

This verse is commonly linked to Christ's birth, but the linkage is only understandable to us because we can use the events of history to prove it. But then, that's one of the primary purposes of long-term prophecy: for later generations to verify that God's promises have indeed been kept. For all those who lived before David, Isaiah, and the other prophets, I suspect their immediate understanding was something like, "Yes, that makes sense: a snake normally bites at ankle height, and whenever I see one I smash it over the head."

So just when does the first definitive promise of a Messiah occur? I started searching through all the references I could find regarding prophecy and the Messiah, and I cannot find any specific reference to Christ or a Saviour until some of David's writings in the Psalms. As with the Genesis 3 reference, there are allusions to a Messiah (God's promises to both Abraham and Isaac), but there are no definitive prophecies.

A parallel question arising out of these promises is this: when does the promise of a new Heaven and Earth enter the picture?

And I will make you a great nation, and I will bless you, and make your name great; and so you shall be a blessing; and I will bless those who bless you, and the one who curses you I will curse. And in you all the families of the earth will be blessed.

—Genesis 12:2–3, NASB

This doesn't promise a Messiah at all, except in hindsight. It promises that a nation which will be a blessing to all will come from Abraham's descendants. This same promise is emphasised in Balaam's prophecies (Numbers 24) and by Jacob (Genesis 49).

It isn't until Psalm 2 that we see the coming of the King. And it is as a king that we see Him, not as a spiritual saviour. That prophecy seems to come later.

But as for Me, I have installed My King Upon Zion, My holy mountain. I will surely tell of the decree of the Lord: He said to Me, "You are My Son, today I have begotten You."

—Psalm 2:6–7, NASB

If there's no promise of salvation and no definitive promise of a Messiah to come, then what was the driving force in those early days? The answer to that question is very important in this day and age, because it points towards the manner in which we should be approaching our lives today. So take a moment to work it out. To help in your meditation, ask yourself what Cain, Balaam, Adam, Abraham, Enoch, Moses, and Jesus Christ had in common.

Throwing Cain and Balaam into the equation may at first obscure the answer, but Enoch should be a giveaway because we only know two things about him. Scripture records that he didn't die but was taken by God from this earth. The second fact we know regards the manner of his life: he walked with God. Cain and Adam both were accustomed to talking with God. There are many examples in Scripture of Abraham not only conversing with God but also of being visited by residents of Heaven. Balaam was God's prophet and repeated God's words, implying that he conversed with God. History records that Moses was the friend of God. And finally, of course, is Jesus Christ, who talked with the Father constantly.

With the exception of Jesus, none of the people mentioned were aware of God's plans for our future salvation. None of them knew of the coming Messiah. Abraham, Balaam, and Moses only knew of God's promise of a future blessing to come from Abraham's descendants, yet each person mentioned (with the exception of Cain, who lost the privilege as a result of murdering Abel) lived his life in conversation with God. And that was enough to provide satisfaction.

Much of our evangelism concerns the future. Questions such as "Where will you spend eternity?" dominate our evangelism efforts. Yet the future was not Christ's emphasis. Living in the Kingdom of Heaven was all about living now. Do you remember Paul's words? *"For to me, to live is Christ..."* (Philippians 1:21, NASB). Often we focus on the last half of the verse, but the first half is where we live now.

Scripture doesn't focus on the future, although it does describe it. It also tells us not to worry about it. The Sermon on the Mount was the venue Christ chose to convey this warning, and it's the same Sermon that invites people to become citizens of the Kingdom of Heaven. We don't know how long we will live or what events will take place tomorrow, and we really don't know much about Heaven. What we do know is that the future is known by God Himself. Not even Christ knows when the end will come, only the Father, and yet He is the one telling us to focus on today.

That takes care of the future, but what about today? We shouldn't be trying to sell the future to those whom we encounter. We should be trying to sell the present! In Scripture, long-term prophecy is often linked with prophecy in the short-term. So too our presentation of Heaven should always be linked to the gains to be achieved in this current life. As Paul put it, we should encourage others to follow Christ so that their joy may be full. Coming full circle, the single thing that should make our joy complete is our conversation with God.

Marriage is made complete through the sharing of events, one's current thoughts and future aspirations, and the odd joke with one's spouse. In a much more intense fashion, that same sharing is what makes being a Christian a complete plan for living. Or at least it should. That is God's plan. Heaven is a great future, but we don't live in or for the future. The same thing that proved sufficient for the people of the Old Testament without the promise of a Messiah, or even of Heaven, can prove sufficient for us. Each of them was acquainted with God in an intimate fashion. Each talked with Him. God shared moments with them. He had lunch with Abraham, He was a friend of Moses, and He walked with Enoch. Elijah was so intimate with God that He could see the hosts of angels that were protecting him from enemy soldiers. We have been invited to share the same intimacy.

Something to think about!

Chapter 52

Christmas: The Beginning and the End

CHRISTMAS IS COMING, AND CHURCHES, STORES, HOUSES, AND THE INTERNET are either filled with, or soon will be filled with, stories and memories of Christmas past, good will messages, and best wishes for the holiday season. The temptation for all budding writers, of course, is to compose their own Christmas message. Relax. Don't stop reading, because this is not a Christmas story.

Have you ever worked on one of those gigantic 1500-piece jigsaw puzzles? The neighbours up at the cottage we visited as kids were committed to puzzles. The latest effort sat on the table in the sitting room, attracting each passerby to pause, reflect, and attempt to fit one more piece into the gradually expanding picture until finally a marathon effort revealed the complete landscape, sailing ship, or whatever. Always, the last piece was put into place with a shout of triumph and loud cheer.

From the moment Adam disobeyed, God has been fitting together an enormous picture called "Redemption." To achieve the end result, He selected a man from Ur and moved him and his family over two thousand miles. The descendant of a prostitute from Jericho became the second king of Israel. He caused hungry lions to skip breakfast and enabled a boy in a psychedelic coat to eventually become the second most powerful man in Egypt.

Following His birth in a stable, He came to live on earth as the apparent son of a carpenter. He spent three years as an itinerant rabbi and finally was falsely accused, arrested, tried, convicted, and sentenced—all within a few short hours. He was whipped, stripped, mocked, and marched through the city streets until finally, on a desolate hilltop, He was barbarically executed. Then came the final crescendo and a single loud cry: "It is finished!" God had conceived the plan, working out every single detail. He had chosen the time, place, family, birthplace, courthouse, and place of execution. No detail was too small.

What is the point? Simply this! Each of us knows of someone or some group who is trying to fit an additional piece into God's puzzle. It won't work and the piece won't fit. God warned us that people would attempt to improve on His plan through the authors of practically every book in the New Testament. And since those days, we've had countless cults ranging from the Jehovah's Witnesses to the Christian Scientists, from the Church of Scientology in the twentieth century to Mohammed in the fourth century. They're all trying to add something to God's plan.

There is no place for human works in God's salvation. There is no adjusting the border or reworking the corners to permit us mere mortals to add anything. All we can do is admire the final result and accept it, just as it is. Get it? Dying to save someone's life doesn't help, and stealing the crown jewels won't hinder. This is the greatest Christmas gift we can offer to our friends and neighbours: the keys to the Kingdom of Heaven. Christ unlocked the gates and threw them open for us to accept on Easter morning. When He cried, "It is finished," the last piece was in place. And it all started on Christmas morning. The true meaning of Christmas is found in the events of the cross.

Something to think about!

Chapter 53

Joy at Christmas (Even When There Is Nothing to Be Joyful About)

The angel said to her, "Do not be afraid, Mary; for you have found favor with God. And behold, you will conceive in your womb and bear a son, and you shall name Him Jesus."

—Luke 1:30–31, NASB

IT IS A WELL-KNOWN PASSAGE. EVERY CHRISTMAS, WE READ THESE wonderful words the angel spoke to Mary, telling her that she has been chosen to be the mother of the Messiah. She has found favour with God. So what happened next?

Now at this time Mary arose and went in a hurry to the hill country, to a city of Judah, and entered the house of Zacharias and greeted Elizabeth.

—Luke 1:39–40

Mary was in a hurry. As soon as she discovered she was pregnant, she got up and ran to visit her cousin, abandoning her betrothed husband, her family, and any responsibilities she may have had. She fled for her life and for the life of her unborn child. Jewish law was very clear about what her fate would be should the neighbours discover she was pregnant.

Because of his deep fear, King Herod had ordered the construction of a series of fortress palaces (they were both for defence and his own creature comforts) to guard his own body in the event of insurrection or an assassination attempt. They stretched from north of the

Sea of Galilee (Caesarea Philippi) to the deserts south of Jerusalem. Theses fortresses were positioned a day's ride apart to ensure Herod's safety at night, regardless of where in his kingdom he was visiting at the time. Joseph was a skilled craftsman, and one of these fortresses was located close to Nazareth. It is likely, therefore, that Joseph was employed on the construction project and was away from Nazareth for weeks at a time. The townspeople would have known it wasn't possible for Joseph to be the father and would have likely arranged the execution of Mary to preserve his honour and that of the town.

> *If a man be found lying with a woman married to an husband, then they shall both of them die, both the man that lay with the woman, and the woman: so shalt thou put away evil from Israel. If a damsel that is a virgin be betrothed unto an husband, and a man find her in the city, and lie with her; then ye shall bring them both out unto the gate of that city, and ye shall stone them with stones that they die; the damsel, because she cried not, being in the city; and the man, because he hath humbled his neighbour's wife: so thou shalt put away evil from among you.*
>
> —Deuteronomy 22:22–24, KJV

So Mary fled. She had found favour with God, yet she ran for her life. What's wrong with this picture?

Mary stayed with her cousin for about three months and then travelled home. It is unlikely that she had heard any news from her betrothed during the time she was away, and it is definite from the angel's visit to Joseph that he was unaware of her condition. Imagine his reaction when he first met Mary upon her return. What do you say to a pregnant spouse when you know it wasn't you who was responsible for her condition? When we read that Joseph, being a just man, was going to divorce Mary privately, we're reading about the best news Mary could have expected at that juncture. Again, turning to Deuteronomy 22, we read,

> *If any man takes a wife and goes in to her and then turns against her, and charges her with shameful deeds* and publicly defames her,

and says, "I took this woman, but when I came near her, I did not find her a virgin... But if this charge is true, that the girl was not found a virgin, then they shall bring out the girl to the doorway of her father's house, and the men of her city shall stone her to death because she has committed an act of folly in Israel by playing the harlot in her father's house; thus you shall purge the evil from among you.

—Deuteronomy 22:13–14, 20–21, NASB (emphasis added)

This was God's law as given to the Jewish people by Moses. Scripture records that Joseph was not going to go to the elders; he was a good man, but it still left Mary with no visible means of support in a country where a single mom was considered to be a prostitute. Yet she had found favour with God?

Six months later, Mary gave birth to her son and put him to bed in a feed trough. By now she certainly must have wondered whether not having found favour with God would have been a better option.

And so we could continue through her life as the mother of Christ. Certainly there would have been periods of joy, but she knew from the outset that her Son was born to die. On that day, she stood at the foot of the cross whilst the majority of His followers cowered out of sight of Golgotha; four women and one apostle were the only friends Jesus had left to stand by His side through those last pain-filled hours. Even His brothers had abandoned Him.

Therefore the soldiers did these things. But standing by the cross of Jesus were His mother, and His mother's sister, Mary the wife of Clopas, and Mary Magdalene. When Jesus then saw His mother, and the disciple whom He loved standing nearby, He said to His mother, "Woman, behold, your son!" Then He said to the disciple, "Behold, your mother!" From that hour the disciple took her into his own household.

—John 19:25–27

Some years later, it's likely that Dr. Luke interviewed Mary to confirm details for the biography of Christ he was writing for the church. Mary's remarks regarding her thoughts are recorded in Luke 1:

And Mary said: "My soul exalts the Lord, and my spirit has rejoiced in God my Savior. For He has had regard for the humble state of His bondslave; for behold, from this time on all generations will count me blessed. For the Mighty One has done great things for me; and holy is His name."

—Luke 1:46–49, NASB

Many of you have endured some form of trouble over the past year. For some, it has been the death of a dear friend or relative. For some, it has been the loss of a job or financial trials. For others, there has been war, floods, famine, and disease that has threatened your family or nation. I doubt, though, if any of us have endured the pain and suffering that Mary went through.

We consider Christmas to be a joyous occasion, but what if one of those tragedies just mentioned has trapped us in a net of pain? No words I could write can possibly change that pain to happiness, but maybe, just maybe, the words of Mary written so long ago can provide the encouragement you need to go on and maybe even smile a little. Her own future was uncertain, as it was quite possible the town would stone her. Scripture said that her son would die. She was alone and unsure whether her betrothed would protect her or cast her out, yet she said, *"My soul exalts the Lord, and my spirit has rejoiced in God my Saviour"* (Luke 1:46–47, NASB).

These are triumphant words of pure joy. The only ones that match it are those heard on Easter morning: *"He is risen, He is risen indeed."*

Something to think about!

Chapter 54

Some Not So Common Sense

FIRST A DISCLAIMER: THERE IS NO METHOD KNOWN TO MAN WHEREBY THE age of the earth can be proven. For both creationists (young earth) and evolutionists (old earth), when all is said and done, the age of the earth is very much a matter of faith. There's no outside reference clock to which events on earth can be tied, so whatever your belief, it starts with an assumption that cannot be confirmed. If I, as a creationist, discover something that doesn't fit with my own particular bias, I can either make excuses for it or write it off as one of God's mysteries which I am not meant to understand.

Here are two seeming contradictions, one from each side. Scientists have discovered soft tissue in dinosaur bones, when it is known that soft tissue cannot survive the time period between the age of dinosaurs and now. Creationists cannot explain the presence of light originating from stars many more light-years away than the presumed age of the earth.

In other words, determining the age of the earth or the stars isn't really a matter of scientific observation, nor can it be subjected to scientific experiment. Rather, when all is said and done, it's nothing more than a debate (sometimes very heated) with arguments on both sides based upon that individual's assumptions about the unobserved past.

Scientific Reasoning

Christians should not fear science. In fact, we should be amongst its greatest supporters, for pure science is nothing less than the pursuit of a greater truth through an experimental process. For several centuries during the Middle Ages, the church provided scientific leadership. The disenfranchisement between the church and science is recent history and has its roots in man's attempts to eliminate God from society.

Scientific reasoning is the foundation supporting the entire structure of logic which underpins scientific research. There are four basic pillars that support the scientific method.

1. Observation

Most research has real-world observation as its initial foundation. Looking at natural phenomena is what leads a researcher to question what's going on, and to begin to formulate scientific questions and hypotheses. Any theory or prediction will need to be tested against observable data.

2. Theories and Hypotheses

This is where the scientist proposes the possible reasons behind phenomena, governed by the laws of nature. In his endeavour to arrive at a reasonable explanation, the scientist tries to break phenomena into small, testable segments and then proposes various tests or experiments that will either prove or disprove each of these segments.

3. Predictions

A good researcher will predict the results of their research, stating their idea about the outcome of the experiment, often in the form of an alternative hypothesis. He then tests his predictions rather than the theory itself. If the predictions don't match the reality of the experiment, the theory is incorrect either in whole or in part.

4. Data

Data is the applied part of science. The results of real-world observations are tested against predictions. Obviously, if the observations match the predictions, it is safe to say that the theory is strengthened. If they don't match up, the theory stands in need of correction or elimination.

Each of the following is a published observation made by scientists. None of these observations can be used to prove that the earth is of any particular age. When applied against the scientific principles outlined above, they all fail in one particular manner: they are not provable. But they do provide a strong argument against those who declare that evolution is a settled science. Read along, apply the four basic pillars of scientific reasoning as you read, and see what you think!

Things that Don't Add Up

1. The internet, or, for those who prefer more traditional reference sources, a good encyclopedia, has a number of photographs of a creature that is from both the past and present. The earth's fossil record of the coelacanth dates from around 65 million years B.C. Then they seem to disappear until 1938 when chance netting revealed that they were alive and well. The first species of fish is deemed to be 65 million years old whilst the second is less than 50. That is 50 years, not 50 million.

   The problems this creates for palaeontologists are actually quite simple and easy for us non-science types to appreciate. According to palaeontologists, the earth's fossil record contains specimens dating from a few thousand years through to the hundreds of millions. Through that fossil timeline, they endeavour to trace the development of different species through skeletal changes. Very simply, the deeper in the ground a fossil is discovered, the older it is assumed to be.

   The youngest coelacanth specimen (that's the fish's official name) is dated around the sixty-five-million-year mark. Then they vanish until they were discovered alive and well in 1938. So, where were they hiding? You would think that somewhere in that sixty-five million years, at least one fish would have died and been buried amongst the other newer fossils, but it didn't happen.

Even worse from an evolutionary perspective is the absence of change. For all intents and purposes, the skeletal structure and size of the modern living variety is identical to that of the fossilized one. This is truly amazing. Whole species have developed and become extinct, and the early primates have matured, divided, and given rise to the great apes (and of course man) whilst this unloved and unnoticed specimen has soldiered on, unchanged.

Prior to the discovery that the coelacanth was alive, it was believed that descendants of this family transitioned into amphibians and eventually emerged from the seas. Their fossilized fins had a unique bony structure that was believed to be suitable for "walking" along the sea bottom, providing the mobility needed for those descendants to travel upon land. Since then, however, scientists have determined that the coelacanth is unable to survive for any length of time in the upper levels of the oceans: they are a bottom fish, requiring the higher pressures of the deep, so they are probably the least likely candidates for transition, and indeed, palaeontologists have dropped them from consideration as a missing link.

2. Geologically speaking, Australia is a relatively stable country. Its predominate features are believed to have been recognizable in their present form for a long, long time. Indeed, Lake Eyre, a salt lake, is dated to the later stages of the Tertiary Period (about two million years ago), when much of central Australia was warmer and wetter than now. It is believed by archaeologists to have been covered by rain forest. But when the salt accumulation in the lake was quantified, researchers were horrified to discover that, given an average flooding interval of fifty years, there was only seventy-three thousand years worth of salt.

Further research made it even worse. Locals affirmed that the average interval between floods was only eight years, meaning that the total amount of salt on the lakebed represented only about twelve thousand years. Somehow, 99.9% of the salt that should be there isn't, and scientists have no explanation. Twelve thousand years does happen to fit within the parameters for a catastrophic geological event that rearranged the water flows and caused significant climate change (a global flood), but that possibility is never considered.

3. Scripture declares that the Heavens are God's source for advertising. Besides, we are all fascinated by the vastness of space. I guess there's a little Buck Rogers in each of us.

In the last half-century, the distance from the earth to the moon has increased by two meters, or by four centimetres per year. This also implies that the movement of the moon around the earth has slowed ever so slightly. The cause is attributed to tidal friction. Now, it may not seem like very much—and it isn't—but the moon is supposedly 4.5 billions of years old. If it has recessed at the same rate for that entire period of time, this would indicate that when formed, the moon was only 162,000 kilometres from the earth. If this had been the case, supposing that each celestial body could withstand the gravitational force being exerted on it by the other without being pulled apart, high tide would have flooded all of North America east of the very highest peaks of the Appalachians, and all of Europe north of the Alps, each and every day. The land would have been scoured clean by the sheer force of the water flowing in and out. It isn't plausible and it doesn't fit with the known facts regarding the geological history of our planet.

4. Methane (CH_4) breaks down under the impact of UV radiation. Titan, one of Saturn's moons, has an atmosphere that supports huge clouds of methane, a gas that should have been obliterated by the sun's UV rays a long

time ago. What should be visible are lakes of liquid ethane with the freed hydrogen having escaped into space. Titan's gravity is too weak to retain a grip on free hydrogen. The quantities measured are consistent with a geologically young Heaven.

Conclusions

These are only a few of the known facts that call into question society's commitment to evolution. However, there are no proofs that can confirm the correct version of events. That is up to the individual. The evidence listed above places realistic doubt on the history of events as taught in today's science classes, but in the end it is up to you to believe.

Throughout these pages, we have thought about God and our position in the Kingdom of Heaven. We have considered creation, miracles, relationships, and prayer. It is all one package. It really isn't possible to reject Genesis 1 and accept the promises of John 3 in total faith.

The concept of evolution was formalized in the mid-nineteenth century by a man. Creation was conceived in the mind of an almighty God and then spoken into place. That same God reaches out in love and offers us eternity. Your call!

Something to think about!